From Son of Sam to Son of Hope

THE AMAZING STORY OF DAVID BERKOWITZ

RoxAnne Tauriello

ISBN 978-1-64569-605-6 (paperback)
ISBN 978-1-64569-607-0 (hardcover)
ISBN 978-1-64569-606-3 (digital)

Christian Faith Publishing, Inc.
832 Park Avenue
Meadville, PA 16335
www.christianfaithpublishing.com

Disclosure: David Berkowitz receives no compensation from sales of this book.

Printed in the United States of America

"I have known David Berkowitz for well over twenty-five years, he is the real deal. A man who knows firsthand the power and forgiveness of the Lord Jesus Christ."

—Rev. Tony Loeffler, President of The
International Solid Rock, Inc.

"The repentance and conversion of David Berkowitz is none other than a modern-day version of the Apostle Paul's miraculous transformation." Lamentations 3: 22-23

—Rev. Daniel Scanish, Pastor of Sayre Woods
Bible Church in Old Bridge, New Jersey

"My understanding of saving grace has been deepened by seeing what Christ has done in the heart of David Berkowitz."

—A. Troy Thomas, Director of *Forgiven for Life*

"The spiritual transformation of David Berkowitz from 'Son of Sam' to 'Son of Hope' is truly the work of God seen in a person's heart."

—Rev. Tom Detamore, Pastor of Ardena Baptist
Church in Freehold, New Jersey

CONTENTS

Introduction

From 1976 to 1977, New York was gripped in a state of near panic as mass murderer David Berkowitz, labeled "Son of Sam", was involved in a reign of terror on the streets of New York, resulting in six brutal murders and seven others critically wounded.

Today he is serving six life sentences. Until now, the media and general public has only centered on his past, but as horrendous as his life was then, there is more to tell—much more! Who is David Berkowitz today?

Now, for the first time, RoxAnne Tauriello, a close friend of David Berkowitz since 1993, reveals through a multitude of personal visits, letters, and phone calls, his amazing journey from "Son of Sam" to "Son of Hope", revealing that if God can forgive and change a former arsonist, Satanist, and serial killer, then God can forgive and change anyone upon repentance and faith in Jesus Christ.

CHAPTER 1

Why Not David Berkowitz?

The van with all our equipment inched past the guard tower. High above, the guards of the Sullivan Correctional Facility scrutinized every move. High fences loomed ahead of us. The bright sun reflected off the steel razor wire, marking the dividing line between freedom and confinement.

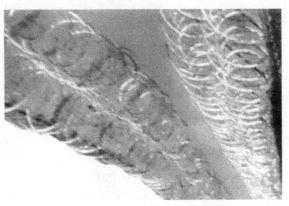

Captured in this picture is razor wire that can cut
a man into pieces, should he try to escape

Trapped in this numbing atmosphere, my mind raced back to a cozy diner long ago. There, a series of events began that would lead me to this moment.

In between sips of coffee, a pastor friend and I chatted about my television program, *The RoxAnne Tauriello Show*, a cable show I had started producing a few years earlier, with the hope of exposing people to the message of the gospel. Soon our conversation drifted to the topic of future guests—the real "talk" of talk shows. Pastor Nash, wanting to be of help, tossed out a name as casually as one might say, "pass the cream."

"Why not interview David Berkowitz, RoxAnne? He's a born-again Christian."

The cup of coffee froze at my lips. "Really?!" The idea of interviewing someone like David Berkowitz, known to most as "Son of Sam," flooded my head with a flurry of thoughts and emotions. "David Berkowitz?" I mused. "A killer turned saint?" The potential impact of such an interview set the gears of my mind into hyper-drive.

Most people, especially those residing in the greater New York metropolitan area, have a haunting familiarity with the "Son of Sam" murders. During the seventies, these horrendous crimes filled the window of every newspaper stand in the city.

".44 Killer: I Am Not Asleep"
"Wanted: Son of Sam"
"No One Is Safe from Son of Sam"
"Killer to Cops: I'll Do It Again"
The greatest city in the world was brought to its knees.

The horrific onslaught that began on July 29, 1976, created a wake of devastation. Six innocent young people murdered in cold blood. Seven other people were wounded and emotionally scarred. Most of the victims were teenagers. Numerous families were left grieving, angry, and confused. There were no explanations...no answers...no reasons for this merciless rampage.

On April 14, 1977, the New York City Police Department created the "Omega Task Force," an investigative team that was, at the time, the most comprehensive and expansive search operation in the entire history of the New York City Police Department. More than $90,000 a day was being spent, while 75 full-time detectives and 225 patrolmen joined in the search for the satanic killer who was blanketing the city with an atmosphere of fear and hysteria. The police investigated 3,167 suspects to no avail.

They consulted experts in almost every field—psychologists, psychiatrists, numerologists, biorhythm specialists, hypnotists, and even exorcists. Meanwhile, five thousand calls a day flooded the precinct phone lines, as operators worked around the clock to sort out the various tips and to calm frantic callers. No stone was left unturned in the hunt for the mass killer, the feared "Son of Sam."

A frenzied mood pervaded the police precinct. As time passed and the death toll climbed, a mixture of desperation and determination set in. Exhausted officers of all ranks pushed on, knowing that the one who put this senseless psycho behind bars would not only rid the streets of a menace, but would also earn a well-deserved day in the spotlight, and an almost certain promotion.

On May 26, 1977, the New York City police commissioner released a psychological profile to the public, describing the killer as "neurotic, schizophrenic and paranoid." He also noted that the killer "may quite possibly regard himself as a victim of demonic possession..."

It is hard to imagine the bustling metropolis of New York City brought to a virtual standstill, and the "in your face" New York spirit cowering in fear. Yet the facts speak for themselves.

As the manhunt continued, merchants throughout the city lamented the vacant aisles in their stores at night. In the Queens area, restaurants normally packed and overflowing with people had tables to spare and crates of food spoiling in their kitchens. Discos that normally drew hundreds on Friday and Saturday evenings played to empty dance floors. And bands scheduled to play found themselves in the unemployment line.

Beauty parlors, on the other hand, had an explosion of business. Since most of the victims were brunette, young brunettes across the city lined up to have their hair dyed blonde in hopes that the deranged killer would not look their way.

The New York nightmare, however, would come to an end on August 10, 1977. A simple parking ticket left on a car would lead police to the home of a tormented postal worker named David

Berkowitz. After terrorizing the city of New York for thirteen months, "Son of Sam" had finally been captured! Following an initial interrogation, the police transported Berkowitz to Brooklyn and booked him for murder and attempted murder.

Undoubtedly, Berkowitz at that period of his life was twisted and perverted in his thinking. By his own testimony, the events of his initial capture and arrest seemed almost comical. In a statement he said,

> "I have never seen anything like it…the photographers were getting their cameras knocked out of their hand—they fell like dominos you know…they were only interested in taking pictures…of anything, even of each other's heads… I have never seen anything like it…it was comical… I saw them all—one of them stepped out of a car and almost got hit. The police even had it hard. They had trouble moving me. They had to push them all away. When I smiled, they said, 'Ah, you see he's smiling—he's happy he did it.'" Reflecting on the scene, Berkowitz adds, "I thought of it as a job. I never was real happy."

The announcement of the capture of "Son of Sam" interrupted television and radio broadcasts across the nation. Around 1:00 a.m. on August 11, 1977, Mayor Beame held a press conference at which time he said,

> "The people of the city of New York can rest easy this morning because of the fact that the police have captured a man whom they believe to be the 'Son of Sam.'"

The police commissioner held up the gun found on Berkowitz. It was later tested and confirmed to be the weapon used in the "Son of Sam" attacks—a .44 Charter Arms Bulldog. During the investigation, the police had attempted to trace the ownership of every .44 Bulldog in the country, an estimated twenty-eight thousand guns, hoping that it would lead them to a clue.

Following the press conference, network news directors frantically rushed to rewrite headlines breaking the news of David Berkowitz's arrest. Camera crews raced into action—everyone wanted their station and news organization to be first to report the story. Within hours, every major newspaper from London to Paris, from Frankfort to Tokyo, had plastered his face on the front page. The *New York Post* had a one-word headline written in bold red letters—"CAUGHT!"

The public was hungry for information regarding David Berkowitz. Who was he? What made him a killer? How did he avoid the searching eyes of the police for so long? News ratings shot up, and sales of daily newspapers in New York nearly doubled. The crimes had ended, but the circus had just begun.

For the next several days, the media fed the public a steady diet of information. News shows devoted major blocks of airtime to the story. Other stories, important and newsworthy, were placed in secondary positions, making way for the sensation of "Son of Sam's" capture. Research teams scanned through mounds of material to recreate Berkowitz's every move in life. Reporters, eager to outdo each other, scurried to Berkowitz's home address in hopes of finding a human interest story, or better yet, someone who knew him and would willingly give any clue or detail to the mystery behind the bizarre murderer. Neighbors, co-workers, even local grocery clerks found themselves in the momentary spotlight.

During his thirteen-month rampage, Berkowitz had been like a night-stalking phantom, and after his capture, the police caught a glimpse of the "madman" through the eyes of photographers and TV cameras. Later he would be locked away at the infamous Attica State Prison, where he remained unapproachable and deadly silent to the mass media.

Then after sixteen years, the serial killer broke his silence and appeared on television's *Inside Edition*. David Berkowitz now said he was no longer a slave to Satan to do his evil bidding. He was set free from sin and demonic oppression through Godly repentance and faith in the shed blood of Jesus Christ, his Savior and Lord. He was now a servant of the living God. Berkowitz also wanted to set the record straight. He revealed that during the "Son of Sam" killings, he had been a part of a satanic cult and claimed not to be the sole shooter. With tears in his eyes, David Berkowitz spoke of young innocent victims slaughtered as offerings for the cult's demonic gods!

This was the man my friend was suggesting I contact! That night I asked myself, "Could it be possible that such a man had actually experienced the transforming power and grace of Jesus Christ? And if David Berkowitz had truly changed, would he be willing to tell his story on my program?"

I was, at that time, very naive about many of the details I have just related concerning Berkowitz's past. But I was not afraid to meet him face-to-face. I had a peace within me and a sense of God's presence that assured me that such a transformation, if true, would be a means of encouragement and hope to many people caught in the darkness of sin and depravity. Despite any challenges I might face in doing this interview, I decided that helping others to see God's amazing love and forgiveness would be well worth the risk.

Even though I felt that God had placed in my heart that David Berkowitz had come to repentance and faith in Jesus Christ, and was forgiven and changed, I still had questions that could only be answered by him. Was his announcement simply a publicity hoax, or even worse, a religious scam to gain sympathy or was this man truly changed? Could the former "Son of Sam" be used as a witness for the gospel, and would he be willing to share God's desire to forgive and change even the most wicked and depraved of people?

I had to find out!

CHAPTER 2

We Have a Plan

I remember thinking back to an evening in August of 1977. It was after dinner, and I was in the kitchen when suddenly the news of David Berkowitz's arrest flashed across the television screen. I breathed a sigh of relief. The nightmare was ending. The police had finally caught "Son of Sam." Cameras flashed as the police rushed him through a sea of reporters. He looked so innocent with his boyish face, blue eyes, and curly black hair. Except for the crazed smile on his face, he seemed incapable of committing such brutal crimes. But there had been no mistake.

In many ways, we are all like icebergs. Much of who we really are is hidden from view, deep beneath the surface. The Bible states this truth another way:

> *"The heart is deceitful above all things, and desperately wicked: who can know it?"* (Jeremiah 17:9, OT)

The only ones who caught an early glimpse of the dark recesses of David Berkowitz's heart were the innocent victims. Tragically for them, it was too late. However, as a Christian TV talk show host, I have met and interviewed individuals who had been set free from the grip of Satan by the transforming power and love of Jesus Christ. Their stories are nothing short of miraculous.

On one show, I interviewed a man who began consuming alcohol at the age of five. His alcoholic mother would often leave half-filled glasses of vodka around the house, which he would quickly find and finish. While his elementary school friends were eating hard candy, he was craving hard liquor. By age eighteen, he was using drugs and quickly became addicted to heroin and cocaine.

As an adult, he became a talented musician, appearing with some of the biggest entertainers in the business. Nevertheless, his addiction continued to haunt him.

Following a drug overdose, he suffered a psychotic breakdown that included seeing and hearing things that were not there. After attempting suicide, he was committed to a state mental hospital. His mind was so far gone that he was unable to put together a coherent sentence. He would often become violent and attack people. In those days, when a patient became uncontrollable, they would be placed in what was known as a "wet sheet pack." The staff would wrap him tightly in cold wet sheets from his ankles to his neck, strap him to a metal table, and give him large doses of medication to calm him down, and keep him from hurting himself and others.

After being released from the hospital, he found himself homeless, living in shelters and sleeping in doorways. He was shuffled in and out of various rehab centers and institutions, but nothing seemed to help.

He was eventually arrested and sent to prison. Still strung out on drugs, he would often be tortured by nightmares. He would lie down in his cell and scream all night in hopelessness and despair as he realized that everyone had given up on him, including his family and friends.

One day while still in prison, he attended a musical program given by a Christian family, where he heard the good news of Jesus Christ. God's offer of forgiveness of sin and a new life, struck a chord in his heart. Crying on his knees, he repented and received Christ as his Savior and Lord. God transformed his heart and mind, freeing him from the chains and bondage of sin, addiction, and mental illness.

Years later, he went on to head up a Christian ministry with the goal of presenting the Word of God and the Savior to former drug addicts and alcoholics, giving them the enabling power to stay clean and sober for the rest of their lives.

Tony on the set of *The RoxAnne Tauriello Show*,
as he gives his testimony

On another program, I interviewed a man named Tony. Sin and "the habit" had caused him to be incarcerated on seven different occasions. His life deteriorated to the point of being homeless, rummaging through garbage cans for food, and going into buildings or crawling behind a piece of plywood to keep warm. Mentally, he was so far gone that even other addicts and criminals were telling him that he needed help.

Tony thought that suicide was a better option than life, until one day while walking the streets, he began to cry out to God saying, "I need help! I don't know who you are, what you are, or where you are. Show me who you are and I'll believe in you from this day forward, and I'll tell people who you are the rest of my life."

Suddenly, a man came out of a building pointing to him saying "Son, do you need a place to sleep tonight?" He invited him into the Salvation Army and gave him a loaf of bread and some baloney.

That day at the chapel service, something supernatural happened. Tony repented and received Jesus Christ as his own personal Savior. God forgave all of his sins and made him into a new creation in Christ. Gone was the drinking and drug use that had destroyed his mind and wrecked his life. Gone was the old sinful lifestyle of stealing from churches and reading tarot cards, and it was all because of repentance and faith in God, his Savior.

Remember Tony's promise to God? "Show me who you are and I'll believe in you from this day forward, and I'll tell people who you are the rest of my life." That's exactly what Tony has been doing, as he ministers to inmates in jails and prisons, singing and praising the Lord.

Tony keeping his promises to God "I'll tell people
who you are", as he sings and praises the Lord

Since 1999, Tony has also been ministering to the disenfranchised people of Cuba and encouraging the body of Christ.

As inspiring as these stories are, I realized from the outset that David Berkowitz was in a far different category. While David's life also had its share of tragedy and misery, the level of pain and suffering he had inflicted on society exceeded anything I had ever encountered. The "credibility issue" of his testimony also demanded scrutiny. Was David Berkowitz truly sorry for his past, or simply sorry for being caught? This question would make this interview much more complex than others. But I also knew that if God's Word could touch the heart of "Son of Sam," then no one was out of His reach.

After learning of David Berkowitz's mailing address, I wrote him the following letter. In summary, it said:

> "Dear David,
>
> Greetings in the precious name of our Savior Jesus Christ. My name is RoxAnne Tauriello. I am a TV producer and host of a Christian television program. I bring people on who are born-again Christians. We talk about their former way of life, how they came to repentance and faith in Jesus Christ, the dramatic change God had made in their lives, and the ministries they are now involved in. The show always has a clear presentation of the Gospel... Would you consider doing an interview program with me? I know that many would marvel at how God can change a person's life... Please let me know if you will allow me to present your personal testimony.
>
> In His precious service,
> RoxAnne Tauriello"

I added this postscript,

> "Please write as soon as possible. Let me know about your ministry. Is there any way that we could speak by phone?"

Along with the letter, I sent him some of my Christian ministry work that included salvation messages I had written for a Christian magazine, as well as Bible quizzes on salvation.

Weeks passed with no response. One day, while at the post office, as people scurried in and out around me, I peered into my PO box. As I slid the envelope out, my eyes began to focus on the name in the return address. "David Berkowitz." I headed back to the car thinking, "What is he going to say? Did he turn down my offer? Is this thing really going to happen?" Sitting in my car, I tore the edge of the envelope open and pulled out the letter.

As I unfolded the crisp paper dated April 5, 1994, I was surprised that the whole message was neatly typed. An aura of professionalism surrounded it. Across the top of the letter were the following words from the Old Testament book of Daniel:

> *"And they that be wise shall shine as the brightness of the firmament; and they that turn many to righteousness as the stars for ever and ever."*
> (Daniel 12:3, OT)

I read on:

"Dear Roxanne,

Greetings in the name of God our Father and in our Lord and Savior Jesus Christ! I am finally getting the opportunity to sit down and send you a letter. Please forgive me for all the time that elapsed. I've been so busy. It seemed that every time I wanted to get a letter out to you something else would come up.

I enjoyed reading and was blessed by your message... Thank you for sharing it with me, and I rejoice in your firm stand on the fundamentals of the faith, of which too many are departing from these days...

I am praying about a future interview on your program. The Lord will have to work everything out;...

In the meantime, I am praying and seeking the Lord's counsel about an interview with you.

Just yesterday, I received in the mail a letter... They asked me to share my testimony

with prisoners in Russia. This is a blessing that
is absolutely beyond what I could ever ask for
or imagine. I have been praying for Russia for
a long time. And now the Lord Jesus is opening
up a door of ministry that is beyond my wildest dreams. This is really where He wants to take
us—BEYOND OUR DREAMS!

Well, I will close for now. I will be in touch
with you… God bless you, Roxanne. Thank you
for writing and sharing.

Yours in Christ,
David Berkowitz"

I put down the letter and stared out in amazement. It sounded
like a letter from a missionary or a pastor! I had to remind myself that
the former "Son of Sam" had written these words.

At the time, I was not aware of the "Son of Sam Letters" on file
with the police. These letters date back to the summer of 1977, and
they reveal a bizarre and frightening personality. For example, one
letter states:

"I feel like an outsider. I am on a different wave
length [sic] then everybody else—programmed
too [sic] kill. However, to stop me you must kill
me. Attention all police: Shoot me first—shoot
to kill or else. Keep out of my way or you will
die!… I am the "monster"—"Beelzebub"… I
love to hunt. Prowling the streets looking for
fair game…and for now I say goodbye and
goodnight. Police—let me haunt you with these
words; I'll be back! I'll be back! To be interpreted
as Bang, Bang, Bang, Bang, Bang—UGH!!

Yours in murder
Mr. Monster"

If I didn't know better, I would have refused to believe that the same person had written both letters. However, from previous experience and from reading the Bible, I knew that such incredible transformations can happen. There is a story in the Gospel of Mark found in the New Testament that illustrates such a truth.

Mark 5:1–20 (NT) states:

> "And they came over unto the other side of the sea, into the country of the Gadarenes.
>
> And when he was come out of the ship, immediately there met him out of the tombs a man with an unclean spirit,
>
> Who had his dwelling among the tombs; and no man could bind him, no, not with chains:
>
> Because that he had been often bound with fetters and chains, and the chains had been plucked asunder by him, and the fetters broken in pieces: neither could any man tame him.
>
> And always, night and day, he was in the mountains, and in the tombs, crying, and cutting himself with stones.
>
> But when he saw Jesus afar off, he ran and worshipped him,
>
> And cried with a loud voice, and said, What have I to do with thee, Jesus, thou Son of the most high God? I adjure thee by God, that thou torment me not.
>
> For he said unto him, Come out of the man, thou unclean spirit.
>
> And he asked him, What is thy name? And he answered, saying, My name is Legion: for we are many.
>
> And he besought him much that he would not send them away out of the country.
>
> Now there was there nigh unto the mountains a great herd of swine feeding.

And all the devils besought him, saying, Send us into the swine, that we may enter into them.

And forthwith Jesus gave them leave. And the unclean spirits went out, and entered into the swine: and the herd ran violently down a steep place into the sea, (they were about two thousand;) and were choked in the sea.

And they that fed the swine fled, and told it in the city, and in the country. And they went out to see what it was that was done.

And they come to Jesus, and see him that was possessed with the devil, and had the legion, sitting, and clothed, and in his right mind: and they were afraid.

And they that saw it told them how it befell to him that was possessed with the devil, and also concerning the swine.

And they began to pray him to depart out of their coasts.

And when he was come into the ship, he that had been possessed with the devil prayed him that he might be with him.

Howbeit Jesus suffered him not, but saith unto him, Go home to thy friends, and tell them how great things the Lord hath done for thee, and hath had compassion on thee.

And he departed, and began to publish in Decapolis how great things Jesus had done for him: and all men did marvel."

Although I had not yet met David Berkowitz, the spirit and words of his letter assured me of the reality of his change. The transformation in his life seemed as real as the one recorded in the Gospel of Mark.

Shortly after receiving the letter from David, I decided to bring it to a barbecue hosted by some of my friends. I wanted to conduct a test. As evening came, we went into the house and gathered in the living room.

"I have a letter from someone very famous," I announced. I didn't use the word "infamous" in order to avoid giving any hints.

I read the letter out loud. Then I asked, "Who do you think wrote this?" Just as I anticipated, they began rattling off names of various well-known Christian speakers. To increase the level of surprise, I placed a yellow sticker over David's signature. I then passed the letter around to each person with the instruction to lift up the sticker and read the signature. I watched their faces as they peered under the sticker and mouthed in astonishment, "David Berkowitz!"

The incredulous looks on their faces once again confirmed in my mind and heart that his amazing story needed to be told. I considered his letter so powerful that I wrote him requesting permission to read a part of it on my program. He wrote back:

"Dear RoxAnne,

Greetings in the name of the Most High God and His Son Jesus Christ!

Please feel free to use any and all portions of any letters and previous correspondence you may have received from me. You have my express permission to utilize anything from me that will serve to glorify Christ and give Him honor and glory.

I am so thankful that the Lord has given me the task of ministering to the men behind prison walls who are emotionally disturbed and troubled. This is truly a blessing.

The outreach to Africa is also going well, although it is small. I wish that I could share with you some of the correspondence I got from Ghana and Tanzania. In fact, I do have a copy of one recent letter from a woman who operates a Christian Children's Orphanage. But there is so much to be done. Please pray. God bless you and I will be in touch.

Yours in Christ,
David Berkowitz"

I wrote David back, thanking him for the use of his material. Then, on February 14, 1995, he wrote me the following letter:

"Dear RoxAnne,

May the Lord bless you and your family in a unique and special way. I have your letter and I want to thank you for writing. Thank you for being patient with me. I felt the need to pray and seek the Lord's direction before answering and making a decision.

RoxAnne, I am very pleased with all that you shared about your TV ministry. I think it is a blessing that you are serving the Lord this way, that you have a passion for souls and also warn others that there is a literal hell. May Christ continue to strengthen and anoint the work.

I also appreciate your many words of comfort and encouragement. Thank you for your prayers for me, and I am doing likewise for you.

Yes, I am willing to do a program for the Lord's glory. I am more than happy to do this…

I will close for now. May the grace of God and the love of the Lord Jesus Christ, and the fellowship of the Holy Spirit be with you always.

Your Brother in Christ,
David Berkowitz"

I couldn't believe my eyes! I reread the letter several times to make sure I had not misinterpreted it. "Yes, I am willing to do a program for the Lord's glory…" I let out an inner shout of joy. The interview I had prayed for was becoming a reality.

But now, strangely enough, reality began to affect my dreams. I tossed and turned in my bed several nights in a row as nightmares of death flashed through my mind.

In one nightmare, I am in a garage. I look up and see a car dangling over my head. As I dodge out from underneath it, the car begins to swing. Faster and faster it swings and I run from side to side, trying to escape the blows.

In another nightmare, my mother and I are in the kitchen. Suddenly I turn and see our cat, lying on the kitchen floor—decapitated. A pool of blood surrounds her body. Blood is splattered across the kitchen counters and cabinets.

Other dreams cast me into a world where I am stalked by a lion or drowning in a flood. After each successive dream, I found myself sitting straight up in my bed staring into the darkness, and realizing that these nightmares were satanic and that there were evil forces trying to stop my ministry with David. Undeterred, I continued to trust in God and move forward.

To film the interview with David Berkowitz, my next step was to gain the approval from the prison authorities. Interviewing someone like David Berkowitz can be complicated due to the security precautions, but surprisingly, the state and prison officials not only consented to my request but also treated me graciously. The same God Who opened the prison doors for the Apostle Paul to get out, was opening similar doors for me so that I could get in.

On March 23, 1995, David wrote another letter. The heading quoted a New Testament passage from the book of Romans:

> *"But God commendeth his love toward us, in that, while we were yet sinners, Christ died for us."*
> (Romans 5:8, NT)

It continued:

"Dear Sister RoxAnne:

Greetings once again in the name of our Wonderful Lord and Savior Jesus Christ! I have not heard from you since your letter back in early February. RoxAnne, I want to encourage your heart and let you know that I am most excited about the opportunity to do the program. Let God get all the glory."

As I read his words, my heart sank. I had gone on vacation and had forgotten to tell him. David continued his letter, instructing me on what to do:

"May I suggest that you make sure that the list of people who are to come in be sent to him as soon as possible, as well as a complete list of all the equipment you want to bring in…kind of like an inventory list…

Please leave New Jersey as early as possible because it will take a good while for all your people to clear security at the front gate. Each piece of equipment has to be inspected for drugs and weapons. So be prepared for some administrative delays. Nevertheless, the Lord shall clear a path.

Lord willing, we shall meet soon. I thank Him so much for the privilege to share my testimony. Let's join together in prayer that souls are saved and hearts encouraged to seek the Lord Jesus. Maranatha!

In Christ,
David Bro. David"

On March 29, 1995, almost a year after my first letter from David, he called me for the first time. It is fascinating how much one can learn about someone simply by reading their letters. Already, to a great degree, I felt I knew this man. Yet up to now, we had never spoken. What would it be like to talk to him? Would his voice convey the same sense of joy and sincerity that was reflected in his letters?

When the expected call came in, I answered the phone, and on the other end of the line, I heard "God bless you, RoxAnne!" The sound of David's voice exuded warmth and genuineness. I was put at ease immediately.

As our conversation proceeded, it became evident that David's heart cry was for God to be magnified and not himself. He wanted the interview to focus on God's love and mercy in forgiving a former arsonist, Satanist, and murderer. "Now, RoxAnne, we're going to lift up the name of Jesus!" he exclaimed enthusiastically.

"Yes, David," I answered, "That is exactly what we will do."

I took the lead in planning the interview. "Now, David, in the beginning, we will need to spend some time discussing your past crimes."

I sensed a silent tension on the other end of the phone. David's past was almost unbearable for him to relive. But we both knew that the brightness of David's love for Christ became even brighter when painted against the dark backdrop of his early life.

Even as a child, demonic forces plagued David. His childhood years were strange, to say the least. While most children fear the darkness, David hungered for it! He often secluded himself under his bed or in his closet for hours at a time. Malignant forces would drive him into the darkened streets where he would roam around for hours. As early as ten years of age, David was so tormented that he contemplated suicide.

Our interview would also need to resurface the deep depravity of David's past. However, we both agreed that our discussion would not end on such a negative note. We had a wonderful message that the world needed to hear. "Son of Sam," through God's forgiveness and transforming power, was now "Son of Hope."

During the interview, I also needed to ask David some hard questions to convince viewers that he was not a religious charlatan, but a man with a true understanding and knowledge of God's Word. I would pose the following questions to him:

- When you committed those terrible crimes, were you aware of a coming Day of Judgment where you would stand before a Holy and Righteous God to give an account of every evil thought, word, and deed?
- Do you believe that hell really exists—a place of everlasting punishment and separation from God?
- What do the words love, mercy, and grace mean to you?

As our conversation ended, it was obvious that we had, as they say, "a meeting of the minds." We were convinced that the interview would not only come to pass, but it would also be a great testimony to the immeasurable love and mercy of God through Jesus Christ.

CHAPTER 3

Behind Prison Walls

On March 30, 1995, the day after our phone call, David wrote me saying…

"I am as anxious as you are to do this project, to bring our Savior glory, and to help Him bring in a final harvest… I am in agreement with you concerning the areas you want to discuss. The message should be on salvation. Let us reach the lost… My heart is heavy over all those who are lost."

He closed with the words,

"Be courageous and go forward in the power of the Holy Spirit. Yours in Christ, Bro. David Berkowitz."

Four days later, David called me again to encourage me and to provide some last-minute instructions.

"Have your car checked out, fill it with a full tank of gas, and make sure you leave early."

I wasn't concerned about our car because it never gave us any problems. As for leaving early, we were planning to leave our house at 5:00 a.m. The trip to the prison facility would take a few hours, and we needed to allow extra time to be processed in and cleared by the prison officials. The day before we left, David called once more with words of encouragement.

The day of the interview, April 6, 1995, arrived at last! And I still had not finalized the questions I was going to ask David during the interview. The details of arranging everything had pulled my mind in other directions. Finally, at two o'clock that morning, I was ready. On the counter before me rested a stack of index cards filled with questions and basic information about David. The cards represented a final summary of a multitude of thoughts and ideas for the interview. Leaning back in my chair, I reflected on how infamous "Son of Sam" was to the world. Silence permeated the air as my exhausted mind continued to churn. "What will tomorrow be like? Will everything go as planned? Will the alarm go off?" My husband was already sleeping peacefully. What a wonderful companion. He never resented the long hours I spent on various projects and television interviews. In fact, he was my right-hand man, assisting me in getting everything ready, and supporting me in those early days of preparation for David's interview. We shared a common goal and vision: to bring the good news of Christ to a needy world.

Of course, not everyone lined up to join our cheering section. Going to a maximum-security prison for an interview was not their idea of a welcome assignment, and televising a program with "Son of Sam" brought its own carload of controversy. One friend's advice was short and to the point—"be careful!" I could amen that advice. I am one who instinctively looks both ways before crossing an intersection. But I have learned over time that there is a big difference between being "careful" and being "fearful." My faith assured me that God had led me to this point and I trusted Him. Praying for His will to be done, I drifted off into a couple of hours of much-needed sleep.

It was still dark when the alarm clock woke us up. My husband rushed to get dressed. My director, John, who had slept on the living room couch, began to gather together all of our equipment. Soon, another member of our crew pulled up into the driveway. Time was precious.

My husband, along with the crew, quickly loaded our car and another van with cameras, tripods, microphones, and all the usual paraphernalia. Despite our lack of sleep and the pressure of details, the adrenaline of the moment kept us excited and alert. With the van and car packed, we hit the road with the anticipation of soon coming face-to-face with the former "Son of Sam."

In the car, I faced another challenge—fixing my hair and putting on my makeup! With one eye fixed on a small mirror, and the other on the lookout for unexpected bumps, I began to make the transformation from a bobby pinned plain Jane, to a hair-sprayed, bright-eyed, camera-ready talk show host. Ah, the wonders of a little paint. I closed my makeup case and began to relax. Things were moving along just as we had planned.

Then, going up a long hill, the car began to vibrate. Bouncing in my seat, I turned toward John who was driving. "What's all the shaking?" He shrugged his shoulders. The car seemed to be going crazy! A few seconds later, the engine stalled. Mercifully, we were able to coast into a nearby gas station.

"What's the problem?" we anxiously asked.

The answer came quick enough. "Engine's blown."

"The engine's blown?" I asked incredulously. "Why today of all days?"

I have never been one of those Christians who claim that if you "just love God" He will take away all your problems. I cannot find that in the Bible and I certainly don't find that in my life. What I do find to be true is that God will get us *through* our problems. He rarely takes us *around* them. Even the children of Israel had to go through the desert before they reached the Promised Land.

Still, I was shaking my head at the news. Here was the most important interview of my life and the car "that never gave us any problems" breathed its last breath at a gas station in the middle of nowhere. I wondered, "Why couldn't the engine blow out on the way to a dentist appointment instead! Is this simply a coincidence, or is someone trying to prevent my interview with David Berkowitz?" I refused to be intimidated or discouraged. We left the car, crammed into the van, and drove away determined to keep our interview. It would take more than a "blown engine" to keep David's message from the world.

Without further incident, we reached Sullivan Correctional Facility, with its tower and loops of razor wire that would cut an inmate to pieces should he try to escape. We now moved into the entrance area where we would be processed in. We were then asked to remove all jewelry and anything else in our pockets and place them in small wooden containers, as the correction officers proceeded to search through our wallets, and other items and equipment, looking for anything that would breach security. This was a typical search for all visitors. Nothing compared to the humiliation prisoners undergo after a visit, where they are totally stripped and examined for any possible drugs or contraband they might have received during a visit. One by one, we passed through the metal detector, as correction officers watched and listened for an alarm to go off, alerting them to anything metal such as a gun or knife. After going through the metal detector, our hand was then stamped and would later be checked as we left the facility to prove that we had indeed been visitors.

The head counselor greeted us and received us very graciously. As we huddled together in a small "holding area," we waited for the door to open. Then, with the correction officer walking ahead, we were taken up a wide cement path into the facility. We crowded into an elevator and went up one floor. Coming out of the elevator, we found ourselves waiting for a large metal door to open electronically. At a designated signal, a buzzer sounded, and suddenly we were in the room where David had given his first and only interview. I would be the second person ever to televise a program with the former "Son of Sam."

The crew began the tedious job of setting up. Mounds of wire were unwound. Cameras and tripods were assembled. Microphones were tested. The correction officer (CO) approached me and asked, "When do you want to see Mr. Berkowitz?" I answered, "As soon as possible."

Looking back, I marvel at the irony of life. I was about to come face-to-face with the man who had evaded the biggest dragnet in New York's history. People feared his presence. Now this very man was on his way to meet me.

The CO left in order to escort David into the room. I used this brief time to finish preparing myself for the interview. Carrying my wardrobe bag, I hurried down the hallway to a nearby bathroom. An inmate sat on a bench, gazing at the floor. Chains were around his wrists, waist, and ankles. I scooted past him and into the bathroom. Locking the door, I used the cramped quarters to change from my traveling clothes into a more professional outfit. I put on a black dress with gold sparkles and topped it off with a black velvet jacket and a gold pin. Even in the cold confines of the prison, I was determined to look my best. Exiting the bathroom and moving past the motionless prisoner, I arrived back at our makeshift set. I sat down at a small wooden table and waited for my "special guest."

After letters and phone calls, David Berkowitz and
RoxAnne Tauriello finally meet face to face

Suddenly, a familiar jovial voice echoed through the prison halls, greeting everyone along the way. "Hi, how are you?" As I looked toward the door, I saw someone whose appearance looked more like a pastor than a prisoner. The incredible changes that Berkowitz had undergone were already obvious with his entrance into the room. Here he was, relaxed and amiable. Few would believe that the former "Son of Sam," the man who terrorized New York for more than a year, would come in spreading warmth and goodwill.

Contrast this scene with "Son of Sam's" courtroom encounter with police officers at his sentencing on May 22, 1978. As David Berkowitz was being escorted into the Brooklyn courtroom, handcuffed and chained around the waist with guards hovering over him, he shouted venomous words and began to kick and bite several officers before trying to leap out of the seventh-floor window. Once officers subdued Berkowitz, he was removed from the courtroom, and the sentencing was postponed for three weeks.

People sometimes wonder, "Were you nervous? What were you thinking?" I was not nervous at all. My initial response to meeting David Berkowitz was one of warmth and excitement. His manner was inviting, just like his letters and phone calls. I distinctly remember noting that his once black curly hair was now replaced with a receding hairline. He had large blue eyes and now wore glasses. But the purpose of this interview was to reveal God's amazing love and desire to forgive and change even the vilest of sinners, and the interview would help to answer the question; was this man changed from within?

Encouraged by David's demeanor, I walked up and greeted him. He asked, "How was your trip?"

I responded, "David, you're not going to believe this, but my car, which never gives me any trouble, died on the way over. The engine blew up!" The look of happiness on his face puzzled me. I thought to myself, "My car is ruined. Why does he look so happy? Did he hear me?" He smiled and said, "RoxAnne, the devil must really be angry! He'll do anything to prevent God's work from going forward." David had interpreted my car trouble on a spiritual level and saw the breakdown as a sign of evil attempting to thwart our interview. But today, Satan would be forced to take a backseat, because his former trophy,

David Berkowitz, would now be held up as God's new creation in Christ.

> *"Therefore if any man be in Christ, he is a new creature: old things are passed away; behold, all things are become new."* (2 Corinthians 5:17, NT)

CHAPTER 4

Face-to-Face

David and I waited for the director's final count as we sat across from each other at a small checkerboard table wearing lapel microphones. Formerly, he'd been an arsonist, a Satanist, and a serial killer. He now sat with a Bible by his side! Ah, the mercy and transforming power of God! Sitting in the room with us was a correction officer. It was apparent to me that David had an excellent reputation in the facility. The officer, though very professional, seemed quite at ease. What a stark contrast to the former "Son of Sam" in 1978, when the headline of the *New York Daily News* read "BERKOWITZ GOES WILD IN COURT," shouting "I'll kill them all" as guards tried to stop him from leaping out of the seventh-floor window.

John and the camera crew were in the final stages of checking lighting, audio, and the settings of various camera angles. Video switching would expedite the flow of the program as David and I could be seen on camera separately, and at times together.

When offered a glass of water David said, "I'm okay. I'm okay."

Clearing his voice, he said, "Thank you, Jesus," a response he often made in gratitude to the Lord for any kindness offered to him. As we sat there, I remarked about the time pressures involved in producing and hosting a television ministry. "Every time I do a show, I'm so happy when the program is over."

"Yeah, right," said David. He laughed and then confided, "I don't feel natural at all." "I know," I said, "it's like stress city. There's a lot to do to get ready, and due to my zeal to serve the Lord, I was under other time pressures and deadlines. Would you believe how much sleep I got? Well, maybe two hours. Two hours probably tops. John, my director, slept at the house last night, and we got up at 4:15 a.m."

Laughingly, I said, "One day I'll be able to sleep the night before like a normal person." David and I were once again laughing together.

Now it was time to consider some of the nitty-gritty details of the interview. Could David remove his glasses, and would he be able to see without them? I was also concerned because the prison administration had limited the number of people I could bring into the facility. Some of the crew had been left behind. The one I'd miss the most was my floor manager. She always held up the cue cards for me. Now I'd be forced to hold some of the questions and other information in my hand. Because the room was small with tight camera angles that at times showed a back view of me, the TV audience would occasionally see some information on the cards. I remember thinking that shoots on the road were surely different from the comforts of the television studio.

As we sat there waiting for the director's final countdown, I said to David, "You know what? I don't like to adlib much. Oh, I've done shows like that… But I really like to have it on the cards…" As I was saying this, David, showing concern, unexpectedly lowered his head and placing his hands together for a few moments, silently prayed. But my concern was that if anything of interest was left out, I'd have the information at my fingertips right there on the cards.

I could see that David was more relaxed so I began to kid around a bit. "I'm just gonna hold them in my hand and when they see I have a lot of cards, that's okay. They'll say, 'You know that girl? She has a lot of cards in her hand. She must've been doin' a lot of homework, or she's got a bad memory.'"

David laughed heartily at my little joke, but then, suddenly turned very serious. "Praise God. Thank you, Jesus… Okay, let's lift up the Name of Jesus. We're gonna lift up the Name that's above every other name."

"Amen," I said, "that's what every program is about—that people will come to repentance and faith. That's what it's all about—the Gospel of Jesus."

David spoke from his heart, "I look out there in society and I see people giving up hope in life, people strung out on drugs, alcohol, and life has lost meaning and purpose. They need Christ so bad. They really do."

Following his lead, I replied, "A lot of people in this world have a terrible life, a lot of tragedies. They don't even think about the horrors that the future holds for them (without Christ)—eternal hell. You know what I'm saying, David?"

As David agreed with me, the director broke in saying, "Okay, here we go. Basically, we're ready. We're rollin', RoxAnne. I'm going to leave it up to you." Then, straightening in my chair, I said, "John, I think I'll look right into the camera and say, 'We're here at the Sullivan Correctional Facility,' okay?"

We were now ready. We bowed our heads and prayed, and then the count began. First out loud with "five, four, three," and then stopped while I silently picked up the remaining count, "two, one." The cameras faded up from black.

> RoxAnne: We are here at the Sullivan Correctional Facility, and joining us is David Berkowitz, formerly known as "Son of Sam."
>
> RoxAnne: David, thank you for allowing us this interview.
>
> David: God bless you, RoxAnne.
>
> RoxAnne: Thank you. David Berkowitz, in 1976, you were involved in a reign of terror on the streets of New York.
>
> David: Yes.
>
> RoxAnne: How many murders?
>
> David: I was charged with six murders.
>
> RoxAnne: Six murders? Also, any people paralyzed?

David: Well, yes, one was—seven people were wounded.

RoxAnne: Wounded, paralyzed, blinded? Basically, some of the women that were murdered, were they strangers?

David: Yeah, I didn't know any of them.

David Berkowitz, formally known as "Son of Sam", tightly shuts his eyes and clenches his hands, horrified as I speak about the person he once was and the evil he had committed

RoxAnne: Okay. Formerly they described you as a savage killer, a homicidal maniac, seeking prey. Did any of the murders have anything to do with your involvement in Satan worship?

David: Yes, they definitely did.

RoxAnne: Would you say that you were living in a very depraved and dark world in those days?

David: Right. I had, um, drifted into Satanism and, at the time, with some other people; we gave our lives over to the devil to be his willing slaves. It was just something that we did, and after a period of time, before I knew it, we drifted off into criminal activities and, uh, it was a whole big mess.

RoxAnne: How old were you when you began this terror of murder in New York, your involvement with others, and what you were involved in?

David: I believe… I believe I was twenty-one at the time.

RoxAnne: Twenty-one?

David: I was twenty-one, right.

RoxAnne: Now, when you were committing murder and other horrible acts of violence, did you ever think about a day of judgment? I mean that one day you, David Berkowitz, would stand according to the Word of God, before a Holy and Righteous God and give an account—

David: Mm-hmm.

RoxAnne: Of every evil thought, word and deed? We're talking about giving an account—

David: Mm.

RoxAnne: About murder, six—

David: Mm.

RoxAnne: About paralyzing people, blinding people—

David: Yeah.

RoxAnne: Starting over a thousand fires. Did any of this ever enter your mind?

David: No, RoxAnne, it never did. I never gave a thought to God's judgment.

RoxAnne: You weren't familiar with the Word of God or what the Bible stated—

David: No.

RoxAnne: Concerning a day of judgment?

David: No, I knew nothing about that.

RoxAnne: So there was no fear of future judgment and punishment?

David: I had no fear of God at the time. I was in total, total blindness, total spiritual blindness. I just didn't care, I just—we had in the group—we just wanted to destroy everything in our path. We were just overcome by that evil force or whatever, and there never was a thought that there would be a Holy God that I'd have to stand before one day. I didn't know those things.

RoxAnne: Now, today you are a born-again Christian. You're a Bible believer.

David: Yes.

RoxAnne: Do you believe, today, in a day of judgment?

David: Yes, absolutely, because the Bible says so.

RoxAnne: And where does the Bible state that?

David: For example, in Revelation chapter 20, in verses 11 to 15 [of the New Testament]. If you'd like me to read this to you, I'd love to.

RoxAnne: Please.

David Berkowitz as he reads from the Word of God, pointing out Revelation Chapter 20: Verses 11 to 15

David: *"And I saw a great white throne, and him that sat on it, from whose face the earth and the heaven fled away; and there was found no place for them. And I saw the dead, small and great, stand before God; and the books were opened: and another book was opened, which is the book of life: and the dead were judged out of those things which were written in the books, according to their works. And the sea gave up the dead which were in it; and death and hell delivered up the dead which were in them: and they were judged every man according to their works. And death and hell were cast into the lake of fire. This is the second death. And whosoever was not found written in the book of life was cast into the lake of fire."* [It] says that right in the Scriptures.

RoxAnne: So what you're telling me is that David Berkowitz, a former murderer—

David: And Satanist.

RoxAnne: Satanist—

David: Mm-hmm.

RoxAnne: Believes today that there is future judgment and punishment for those who do not repent and trust in Christ?

David: Yes, absolutely, yes.

RoxAnne: In those days, you did not believe in eternal hell?

David: Well, I knew—I knew that there was a hell, I just somehow knew.

RoxAnne: What made you think that?

David: Well, because actually at the time I was involved in Satanism and we—we used to worship the god of hell. We used to see the devil as being the prince and king of hell and that we would go with him to just party forever when it came time to die, that we would just live with him in hell, wherever that was.

RoxAnne: Mm-hmm.

David: I really didn't see it as a place of torment, the way the Bible goes into great detail describing it. I just saw it as a place to kind of party and hang out with those that served the devil all their life. That was my naive and ignorant view at the time.

RoxAnne: You didn't see it as a place of torment, misery, woe—

David: No.

RoxAnne: Suffering—

David: Mm-hmm.

RoxAnne: Mentally—

David: No, I didn't understand that. No.

RoxAnne: Physically—

David: No—didn't—never told, never really read the Bible, and uh, I grew up in a Jewish home. My parents were kind of religious, and we never really read the Holy Bible. They believed in God, that there was a God, and we'd go to the synagogue on the high holy days to worship Him, but there was no relationship. I didn't know anything about judgment or anything. We just knew the Ten Commandments and some Bible stories and that was it.

RoxAnne: But today you do believe in an eternal hell?

David: Oh, yes.

RoxAnne: David, have you experienced great sorrow over your past?

David: Yes, absolutely. I've been haunted by it for many, many, many years over the life that

I lived and the things that have happened. You know, I don't know why they happened, just got so involved in the evil. It was just a force at the time that just carried me along and carried some of my friends along, and we just plunged into it, and it was like being in the rapids, going into the water—you know, one of those big waterfalls. You just get pulled along by the current, and there just didn't seem to be a way out. I look back now, after years of incarceration, and I think in horror that that was a part of my life, that that was my life back then, and there's nothing—you know, I just look back. How could I ever undo the past, or change it?

RoxAnne: Mm-hmm. There may be people watching that are contemplating rape, robbery, selling drugs, even murdering someone.

David: Mm-hmm.

RoxAnne: What do you want to tell them?

David: I want to tell them that I believe that what they're really seeking is a relationship with God, a relationship with the Lord Jesus Christ. Many people, they—they're trying to find meaning in life. They're trying to find happiness in life. But the Bible says that Jesus came to give us life and to give us life abundantly, but Satan, he came—he came to lie, to kill, to steal, to destroy, and we have to choose whether—what path we're going to go down. But if we choose Jesus Christ, He's going to give us a life of peace and joy if we repent of our sins and turn to Christ, that He will forgive us of our sins and give us hope and meaning.

And I would urge people not to take that path down to destruction because the Bible says the devil is a liar and a deceiver, and he won't tell you what the final consequences of those actions will be, even more than imprisonment, if they were to be arrested. But really, the ultimate penalty would be death, eternity in hell.

RoxAnne: Now, David, you've come to repentance and faith in Christ, acknowledging your former life of sin, desiring by God's grace to turn away from sin, and you've trusted in Jesus Christ as your personal Savior?

David: Yes, yes.

RoxAnne: Who is Jesus Christ?

David: To me, Jesus Christ is the Messiah of the Jews, and He's my Savior. He's my Redeemer, Who through His blood on that cross—

RoxAnne: Yes.

David: He purchased me for God. I put my faith in His blood, and now I know that my sins are covered.

RoxAnne: That He took the punishment—

David: Yes.

RoxAnne: And the penalty?

David: Yes, yes, yes. He's the One that showed me mercy and forgiveness when man showed me no mercy and was not willing to forgive.

RoxAnne: He is the perfect Lamb of God.

David: Yes.

RoxAnne: Like in the Old Testament—

David: Right.

RoxAnne: When they would come with the animal sacrifice and placing their hand upon the head of the animal—

David: Mm-hmm.

RoxAnne: Confessing their sin.

David: Right, right, yes.

RoxAnne: You came to Jesus Christ as the Jewish Messiah—

David: Mm-hmm.

RoxAnne: Realizing that He was the One spoken of in Isaiah 53 [of the Old Testament]?

David: Yes.

RoxAnne: The suffering servant?

David: Mm-hmm.

RoxAnne: The sacrificial Lamb?

David: Yes.

RoxAnne: And that He, on that cross, took personally for David Berkowitz—

David: Yes.

RoxAnne: The punishment and the penalty—

David: Yes.

RoxAnne: For you—

David: Mm-hmm.

RoxAnne: And your sins?

David: Yes, yes. He was the Passover Lamb.

RoxAnne: Yes. What does Jesus Christ mean to you?

David: To me, Jesus means hope, He means mercy, He means forgiveness, He means love. I just gave my life totally to Him, and I've been serving the Lord now for about eight years, and He's just filled me with a joy and a peace that I have never experienced in the world.

RoxAnne: You're in prison now.

David: Yes. I'm in a maximum security prison here.

RoxAnne: For over?

David: Well, now I've been here close to 18 years—

RoxAnne: And—

David: Incarcerated.

RoxAnne: And your sentence is?

David: Uh, well, I have hundreds of years. I really have natural life is what it comes down to.

RoxAnne: And yet you feel, since you've repented and trusted in Christ, you feel peace in prison?

David: Yes, right.

RoxAnne: Joy?

David: Yes, joy, absolutely.

RoxAnne: Happiness?

David: Yes, yes.

RoxAnne: And purpose?

David: Yes—

RoxAnne: Because of—

David: The Lord has filled my life with purpose.

RoxAnne: Because of Jesus Christ?

David: Yes.

RoxAnne: Let me go back again. What does the suffering of Jesus Christ upon the cross mean to David Berkowitz personally?

David: Well, RoxAnne, to me—it means to me that He paid the penalty for my sins.

RoxAnne: For the murders?

David: Yes, for the murders, yes.

RoxAnne: For over a thousand fires?

David: Yes, yes.

RoxAnne: For maiming people?

David: Yes.

RoxAnne: He paid the price on the cross?

David: Right, right, because I was worthy of the death penalty and I was worthy to die for my participation in those crimes, and others that were with me. They did die. They lost their lives shortly afterward in tragic accidents and things, and, uh, I should have been there, too. I should be in the grave right now but Jesus, when I put my faith in Him, I saw that through His shed blood, that my sins were washed away. It didn't matter what I did in the past that the Lord was willing to forgive me.

RoxAnne: Forgive all those past sins?

David: Yes.

RoxAnne: Present?

David: Mm-hmm.

RoxAnne: And even future?

David: Mm-hmm.

RoxAnne: David, when you hear the word *love*, what do you think about?

David: I think about that God is love and that's the way the Bible describes it.

RoxAnne: Is there a verse that comes to your mind?

David: Well, one is John chapter 3, verse 16 [in the New Testament], which is a verse that I love very much, and get to use often in here as we minister.

RoxAnne: Because you do minister to other prisoners?

David: Oh, yeah, sure, all the time. It says that, *"For God so loved the world, that he gave his only begotten Son, that whosoever believeth in him should not perish, but have everlasting life."* [John 3:16, NT]. And it goes on to say, *"For God sent not his Son into the world to condemn the world; but that the world through him might be saved"* [John 3:17, NT].

RoxAnne: When you hear the word *mercy*, what do you think about?

David: That mercy best describes Jesus Christ, that His mercy toward me, His willingness to extend to me, a murderer—

RoxAnne: Yes.

David: His hand of mercy and to make me a minister, too, and a member of His kingdom. I mean, this is the greatest—the greatest gift ever. God is truly merciful, and the Bible says He delights to show mercy.

RoxAnne: Yes. And when you hear the word *grace*, is there a Bible verse, something that you think about?

David: In Ephesians chapter 2, verses 8 and 9 [NT] the Bible says, *"For by grace are ye saved through faith; and that not of yourselves:* it is *the gift of God: Not of works, lest any man should boast."* In other words, boast in what they do in their goodness. The Bible says that grace, His unmerited favor, has been extended to every person.

RoxAnne: To even David Berkowitz?

David: Yes, to even me, and it's a gift of God, not something that we—that I've ever earned or deserved, but it's something that He wants to give.

RoxAnne: Yes. Now, David, going back, you committed horrible, horrible crimes.

David: Yes.

RoxAnne: Do you really believe that your sins are forgiven?

David: Yes.

RoxAnne: Why?

David: Well, because the Bible says so. The Bible says that if we put our faith in Jesus Christ, that our sins are completely forgiven and washed away, that Christ came to die for the ungodly.

RoxAnne: Is there a verse that directly tells you that?

David: Yes, in John chapter 5, verse 24 [NT] Jesus says, *"Verily, verily, I say unto you, He that heareth my word, and believeth on him that sent me, hath everlasting life, and shall not come into condemnation; but is passed from death unto life."* And He's talking here about not just our physical life—

RoxAnne: Uh-huh.

David: But eternal life, the life of our spirit. And it says here, for those people that are in Christ, there's no condemnation to them anymore. They will never be condemned.

RoxAnne: Right, because Christ took all the punishment—

David: Yes. Yes, that's right.

RoxAnne: And the penalty for you and your sins, for me and my sins—

David: Yes.

RoxAnne: And for all those who will repent—

David: Yes, yes.

RoxAnne: And trust in Jesus Christ.

David: Yes, yes, yes.

RoxAnne: That's what the cross is all about.

David: Mm-hmm,

RoxAnne: It's a place of punishment, punished in your stead and in my stead—

David: Yes.

RoxAnne: In His own body—

David: Mm-hmm.

RoxAnne: So that when we die, we will not be punished in eternal hell.

David: Yes. That's right. That's right.

RoxAnne: You know, David, some people, even though we've talked all this while, some people would say, "Well it all sounds good, but, uh, you know, he probably has that jailhouse religion."

David: Mm-hmm.

RoxAnne: What would you tell them?

David: Well, I would tell them that, even though I'm in the prison house, I serve God with all my heart, and I know that—you know, people are naturally skeptical, and that's okay, but as long as I'm here, I'm going to continue to serve the Lord. I don't know what the future holds for me, but I know that, even in here, the Lord uses me to minister to the men, especially the guys with emotional problems, the developmentally disabled. I minister overseas through correspondence, and the Lord has allowed me to touch many lives, even inside these prison walls. So I want to just go forward no matter what people may say or mock or question. I just want to go forward and serve the Lord with all my heart.

RoxAnne: Right. And also, there are many, many people here in prison, and pastors and evangelists—

David: Yes.

RoxAnne: And missionaries—

David: Yes.

RoxAnne: Radio people that I know, that would attest to the fact that you have truly come to repentance and faith in Jesus Christ—

David: Yes.

RoxAnne: And that you are a totally new, new person in Christ.

David: Mm-hmm.

RoxAnne: David Berkowitz, this has been a real joy for me, to come and to talk to you, and to see what God has done in your life. You've become a new creation—

David: Yes.

RoxAnne: In Christ, and this has truly ministered to my life, and it's brought me joy and happiness in hearing you speak.

David: Thank you.

RoxAnne: And I praise and I thank God that today you are my brother in Christ.

David: Amen.

RoxAnne: Thank you, David.

David: Thank God.

RoxAnne: God bless you, David.

David: God bless you.

We were now ready for the final portion of the program. I had asked David if he would sit alongside me. We faced the camera directly. I wanted the angle shot to be head-on as I made a plea to others to receive God's forgiveness, a brand-new life, and eternal life. I felt that people would take courage as they saw the extent of God's love, mercy, and transforming power in forgiving David Berkowitz, a former Satanist, arsonist, and murderer. We all stopped and prayed. Then, with David by my side, I began the salvation message, saying to those who would be watching:

> "David Berkowitz, formerly 'Son of Sam,' told us that he terrorized the streets of New York, and was a Satan worshiper and a serial killer. David Berkowitz understands the issue of crime. He knows that crime is a matter of sin. Rebellion against God's commandments and laws. But David also knows there's an answer to the prob-

lem of crime and sin. It's repentance and faith in Jesus Christ. Why? Because Jesus said,

'For out of the heart proceed evil thoughts, murders, adulteries, fornications, thefts, false witness, and blasphemies' [Mathew 15:19, NT].

Sin originates in man's innermost being, and if there is to be a change, a total change in a person's mind, heart, and life, it must come from the inside out.

But who is able to bring about such a change? Only God, for *'with God, all things are possible'* [Mathew 19:26, NT]. God can transform a mind clouded with confusion and evil, into a sound and a healthy mind. A heart of stone can become a heart of flesh, and God can give the Holy Spirit the enabling power to overcome sin in your life. God can do this for you and even for the vilest of sinners, even a person like David Berkowitz.

For when David heard of God's offer of mercy and His great love and desire to forgive sin, David Berkowitz listened to the Word of God, and he repented. He desired, by God's grace, to turn away from sin, and to trust in Jesus Christ as his personal Savior.

God forgave David's sins and gave him a new mind, heart, and life, along with peace, hope, joy and purpose for life and living, a personal relationship with God, and eternal life in heaven.

Today, David Berkowitz is paying his sin debt to society, and he should. But he will never have to pay his sin debt in hell because it has been paid in full through Christ's shed blood; His death upon the cross."

I knew that David was in full agreement. But I needed to make one more point. Looking straight into the eye of the camera, I asked this question:

> "What about you? Has your sin debt to God been paid in full? You see, even though you haven't committed horrible crimes, God states, *'For all have sinned and come short of the glory of God'* [Romans 3:23, NT]. Because God is a Holy and Righteous Judge, He cannot bypass or overlook sin. Therefore, the Bible states a day of judgment is coming, when people will stand before God, and give an account of every evil thought, word, and deed. And those who have not repented and trusted in Jesus Christ as their Savior from sin will spend eternity in hell.
>
> What must you do to escape future judgment and hell? What must you do to receive God's forgiveness, fellowship, and eternal life in heaven? You need to REPENT. You need to acknowledge that you are a sinner and that you have sinned in the sight of a Holy and Righteous God. You need to be willing, by God's grace, to turn away from a lifestyle of sin.
>
> You need to BELIEVE that Jesus Christ was and is God the Son and that on the cross, He took God's wrath, the punishment and penalty due to you and your sins. He died, was buried, but on the third day, rose from the dead. And the very moment you come to God with sorrow for your sin and a desire to turn from sin, placing trust in Jesus Christ, God the Son, and His death, burial, and resurrection, God will forgive your sins, past, present, and future. You will know God in a personal way, and you will spend eternity in heaven."

Then one of the crew called out, "It's a wrap." The interview was over. David was smiling and as happy as could be. As for me, I was grasping both arms of the chair, and letting out a long, deep sigh of relief. David exclaimed, "Praise the Lord." Then, lifting up both arms, he cried out, "Hallelujah!" and as we both rose out of the chairs, there was laughter, happiness, and excitement. We had finished the interview and served the Lord.

On that day, I left the prison facility feeling on top of the world. God had granted me His favor in the interviewing of David Berkowitz. I saw a living example of His grace, mercy, and transforming power in the life of one of the most wicked of sinners! Joy overwhelmed me.

I had prayed a certain prayer, not every day, not every week, but every so often, saying, "God, please send me someone who has the gift of an evangelist; someone I could work with, who would be my very best friend." Another thought came to me quite suddenly one day, and so I asked, "Lord, couldn't you save someone the whole world knows; someone that people would be amazed about?" Both of these prayers would be answered in the person of David Berkowitz!

But for now, it would be a time of getting to know one another in Christ-centered fellowship and Christian love. In so doing, we would fulfill the New Testament Scripture of 1 John 3:23,

> *"And this is his commandment, That we should believe on the name of his Son Jesus Christ, and love one another, as he gave us commandment."*

CHAPTER 5

Getting to Know You

Our van pulled out of the Sullivan Correctional Facility around 4:00 p.m. I sat in the passenger seat, speechless, staring out the side window, while my mind began to churn out thought after thought.

"I just interviewed the former 'Son of Sam!' I can't believe it actually happened. What an incredible story. What an incredible testimony of God's grace. *Now* what do I do? What's the next step? How will people respond to this interview? Will they see the power of God, or will Berkowitz's past forever cloud people's opinion of him?"

I realized that most people would be highly skeptical of the transformation in Berkowitz's life. After all, serial killers have an uncanny way of masquerading as harmless individuals, hiding their predatory hearts within a sheep's skin, so to speak. There was Ted Bundy. He was handsome, educated, and personable. Yet underneath his charismatic facade lurched a sadistic psychopath. By the time Bundy's murderous rampage came to an end, he had left a trail of sexual assaults and gruesome slayings that would claim the lives of at least thirty women. Then there was Jeffery Dahmer—a quiet, boyish-looking, somewhat shy individual—the seemingly harmless neighbor down the street who liked to keep to himself. Yet he lured seventeen victims to their death, cannibalizing their remains like an animal after its kill. I knew that many would believe that David Berkowitz was playing a similar game, using a thin veneer of charm to garner sympathy, mislead the media, or perhaps to gain an early parole.

I knew one thing—I wasn't gullible. I had been around the block, and I knew enough not to trust a book by its cover.

And yet there was something different about David Berkowitz. He was genuine, honest, and sincere. It was a sincerity that could be felt more than described. I felt it when he quietly sang hymns during breaks in our interview. I sensed it when we prayed, talking to God as if He were his closest companion. Something inside of me—my gut instinct, my spirit, my womanly intuition, whatever you want to call it—said, "This is for real." I am convinced it was the Spirit of God.

David Berkowitz, as he reads from The Bible, seems as if he's caressing The Word of The Living God that he loves so deeply

I could still picture Berkowitz in front of me: his hands caressing the pages of his well-worn Bible, the joy on his face highlighting his pale yellow shirt, the words of Scripture flowing out of his mouth as if they were the very fabric of his heart and mind.

Were those the same hands that fired a .44 caliber gun? Was this the same face that chuckled at the pain of others, and the same mouth that spewed out senseless profanities? Was this balding middle-aged man the same one who terrorized the streets of New York? Was this well-spoken gentleman the same one involved in the murder of six innocent lives and the blinding, maiming, and wounding of seven others? The contrast boggled my mind.

My stomach soon interrupted my thoughts, reminding me that it was time to eat. Spotting a faded gas station sign in the distance, I asked my husband to pull over.

He waited while I slipped into the store. A strange mixture of emotions surged within me as I walked through the aisles of potato chips and soft drinks. I felt an inexplicable sadness coupled with an adrenaline rush that nearly compelled me to rush up to the store clerk and say, "Guess where I've been? I just interviewed 'Son of Sam!'" Resisting the urge, I composed myself, purchased a tuna salad sandwich and a bottle of orange juice, and headed out the door.

Back on the highway, I once again relived the interview. Despite the newfound joy I witnessed in David's words and actions, one thing was clear. Try as he may, there was nothing he could do to change his past. It would forever haunt him. He would never outrun the bitter memories and pain of his life as "Son of Sam." The name would be frozen in infamy, not only in the newspapers but also in David's mind. All the anger, confusion, Satanism, hallucinations, and murders of his past had been wrapped up and packaged in a box labeled "Son of Sam." To mention the name is to open the box and let those memories once again flood his thoughts. What can a man do with a past like David Berkowitz? There only seems to be three options—sear your conscience, go crazy, or hold on to the forgiveness of God as you gaze upon the repugnance of your sin. I believe that David chose the third option. And as the light of God shined brighter in his heart, it only accentuated the dark hues of his past.

Reflecting back on the interview, I remembered describing his past, "Formerly they described you as a savage killer, a homicidal maniac seeking prey." As I said these words, his head dropped as if a weight of shame suddenly descended upon him. His eyes closed tightly. His lips pressed against each other. Ever so slowly, his head nodded in agreement while his hands clasped together as if holding on for life itself.

In that instant, what mental pictures went flashing through his mind? Did he see snapshots of his victim's faces right before he snatched away their lives? Did he see his father's face, streaming with tears, asking him, "Why, David? Why?" Did he catch glimpses of the families—the moms and dads, the sisters and brothers, the friends and loved ones—huddled together, sobbing and moaning at the gravesides of young lives taken too early?

Suddenly the sadness I felt in the convenience store began to make sense. David's past had been a living wasteland. There was no way to sugarcoat that fact. In the process of destroying the lives of countless individuals, he had destroyed his own life as well. He was the embodiment of sin in its ugliest, vilest, cruelest form. The devastation he caused cannot be measured. Lives were taken, families destroyed, innocence lost.

When word of my interview hit the airwaves and the newspapers, the anguish and anger that lay deep in the hearts of thousands affected by "Son of Sam" awakened. A backlash of emotion slapped me in the face because I dared to mention the change in Berkowitz's life, and even stated that he was "the most beautiful Christian I had ever met" (a position I still hold to this day). Metropolitan radio hosts and callers scoffed at Berkowitz's alleged transformation. Newspapers in half-checked mockery proclaimed words such as "Son of Sam is Now TV Preacher." While others shook their heads in disbelief and anger, refusing to believe that someone so evil could become a godly person.

That statement sums up the crux of the matter. Can an evil man change? Can a serial killer find redemption?

Riding home that day, I knew that David Berkowitz deserved to die. He was guilty of murder. He was responsible for his actions. Yet I also knew in my heart of hearts that he was a new man. He had not put on a show in front of the camera. He was not a charlatan looking for another avenue to grab the spotlight. He was a changed man with a hideous past. Such a change would certainly be a miracle. But I believe in a God who performs miracles. I believe in a God who makes streams of water flow in a wasteland.

Before I knew it, we were home. My husband and I collapsed in our rec room, exhausted and excited from the day's events. Out of the blue, my husband blurted out, *"I wonder if David has any relatives or family to visit him. We should go and visit."*

The words of my husband, Sam: "We should go and
visit", caused he and David to become close friends,
who cared about and respected each other.

Somewhat surprised, I replied, *"You're right, we should go visit."*

Two days later, I found myself sitting at a cluttered desk penning a letter to David Berkowitz. The adrenaline rush of meeting him had still not worn off. My mind kept replaying various images of the interview. Joy kept surging in my heart as I reflected on the simple beauty and stark reality of his faith. I had to write. I couldn't contain myself.

The letter was not exceptionally long. I don't even remember what I wrote. I simply desired to let him know how much his testimony had impacted me.

In a reply, he made a point to encourage me:

> "I know that our Beloved Savior will continue to perform a mighty yet tender work through you, Rox. I was deeply impressed when I first met you; for I noticed how often tears came to your eyes when you were sharing the message of salvation, or when I was reading scripture verses.
>
> It is rare to find someone with a tender heart for sinners, a heart of compassion. Paul had such a heart and this is revealed in his writings (for instance Romans 9:1–3)." [NT]

I reflected back to our interview. At times, my eyes glistened with tears and my voice faltered as I spoke. Hearing David speak, I sensed a change in him that is impossible to put into words. His faith exceeded my wildest expectations. I almost felt like a doting mother hearing my child speak the words that I prayed in my heart he would say.

Over the next six weeks, I came to know David Berkowitz more than I could have ever imagined, thanks to numerous letters and phone calls. The content and character of our communication confirmed to me the reality of the change in his heart. I also came to see David as a serious, reflective man with an infectious love for life, and a sense of humor. On April 18, 1995, he wrote:

> "Dear sister RoxAnne:
>
> Praise the Lord! Greetings in the name of our Lord and Savior, Jesus Christ! I have your letter of 4/8. It was good to speak with you over the phone, Rox. I am so thankful that you love the Lord, that He has brought you and your ministry team to me, that we might work together for His glory.

I was going to write you late last week but a big setback developed. I came down with a very bad case of the flu. The Lord has delivered me. Thank God because some thought it may have been pneumonia. I started to feel ill by early Friday, and was bedridden, for the most part, until this morning. I feel much better and stronger. But it is still in me and I'm sweating bullets. PRAISE THE LORD! This is how I spent my Easter/Resurrection week: shivering in bed and feeling like Lazarus!

Seriously, the way I looked and felt, some who had no faith may have already begun to gather my grave clothes. 'Let's see, what am I going to put on Dave for his funeral?' HALLELUJAH! The Lord brought me through!"

Sick and alone in a prison cell, without loving hands to care for him, he still found ways to praise God's faithfulness and to rejoice in the dregs of life.

This was not unusual. David often found a place for humor in everyday annoyances and difficulties of prison life. Once he began a letter to me with the following paragraph:

"Praise the Lord! It is Saturday morning and I am in here fellowshipping with the Lord, typing you a letter, rejoicing in the Lord, and breathing in lots of second-hand cigarette smoke. What's life without a whole lot of suffering? God is still greater than any problem."

During our phone conversations, he would frequently come on the phone with a big jovial, "Hello, Rox!" It was a greeting I would expect from someone on vacation, not someone spending every day of his life in a maximum-security prison.

Once I asked him, "David, how hard is it to make a phone call?"

He replied, "Imagine thirty-five or forty people all standing around your living room waiting to use the phone." Then we both broke out in laughter.

Though he described the situation lightheartedly, later I learned that his assessment was quite accurate. In some of the prisons I visited, there was an average of two phones in every unit of thirty to sixty men. Each prisoner has a restricted list of people he can call. Each and every person on the list must be approved. The calls must be collect, made at regulated times, and limited to a set amount of minutes. When the time is almost up, a recording comes on stating you have sixty seconds, followed by thirty seconds. The call is then cut off whether your conversation is finished or not.

If one can imagine the verbal (and possible physical) fights that would ensue in a household of thirty people with a single phone, then one can begin to get a small taste of being incarcerated. Inmates I have interviewed have spoken of the phone area as a hot spot, where fights can easily break out, and where a man can get "his wig split" (head cracked open) and a "chair upside his head" over usage of the phone. Some even spoke of needing the backing of a gang behind them and how, when you get on the phone, you need to fight for your time. "If you wasn't strong, you couldn't use it."

Today, with our "smart" phones, email accounts, and social media websites such as Facebook and Twitter, we can't even imagine a world where we do not have the ability to freely communicate with our friends and family. Such was David's world. Yet he would never complain. Not once did I hear him sound off on prison food or sweltering prison cells. Whenever he would describe life behind bars, he would simply say, "Lots of little struggles, Rox."

The struggles of prison life, however, did not drive David into an isolated retreat. He was a man with a heart and a passion to do the Lord's work in whatever way he could. I can remember speaking with a deputy warden at another facility who called his jail "sleep away camp" because of the tendency of many prisoners to waste away their time in slumber. That was not true of David Berkowitz. He served in the local chapel at the prison helping and preaching when needed, conducted Bible studies for the prisoners, participated in an outreach of sending Christian literature to pastors in Ghana and Tanzania, two countries that are in Africa. He also wrote messages of encouragement to Christian congregations around the world and ministered in the mental health unit of the prison. In describing this, David once wrote the following:

> "The Lord has opened up a door in which I minister to the special needs men, those who are mentally challenged. I am the only prisoner in the facility who is permitted to go to the mental health cellblock to work and help. It is the Lord Jesus who's given me His special touch for this unique ministry."

African Pastor hands out ministry Bible studies
on God's Way to Forgiveness of sin, Fellowship
with God, and Eternal Life in Heaven

As the extent of David's service to the Lord unfolded before my eyes, I gasped in amazement. No one forces David to do these things. David serves out of love for Jesus Christ, the One who transformed his heart.

In our correspondence and on the phone, David did not dwell on the things he was doing for the Lord. To him, it was nothing noteworthy considering all that the Lord had done for him.

Once in a letter, David lightheartedly wrote, "I've gotta go, Rox. I have to go put a turkey in the oven." It was his way of saying that he was off to another Christ-centered project. Another time he signed a letter to me with "Bro. David B." While the world would see the "B" as the initial for "Berkowitz," I also saw it as the initial for "Busy." David was always about his Father's business. In that respect, we were like kindred spirits. David wrote to me the words that I could have written to myself:

> "Like you, projects and more projects. We seem to have several things in common. At times I am frustrated that others do not have a fire in their hearts to serve the Lord. I am thankful for the opportunity to work with you. The Lord knows my heart cry for lost souls. That no one perish but all come to repentance and faith in Christ Jesus."

In the weeks that followed my interview with David Berkowitz, I had the opportunity to appear on several live call-in radio shows. My statement that "David Berkowitz was the most beautiful Christian I had ever met," certainly generated a lot of listener response! As I prepared for these radio shows, David Berkowitz, the man who had evaded the press for years, continued to pour out his heart to me and revealed his hope for the interview:

> "I am simply asking Jesus to use everything for His glory. I want nothing else but to please Him. Let us keep praying and humbly ask the Lord to use it all for His glory. RoxAnne, the Lord has sent me a wonderful gift when He sent you. I thank Him for your husband and his concern and prayers..."

In another letter, he offered a prayer for me and for my family, saying these words:

> "I will end this letter for now. I'll be phoning you next week, Lord willing. My prayer for you, your family and co-laborers in the gospel is that the Lord gives you a deep rest for your souls. That all of you would experience a deeper love for others, be they saved or unsaved. And that Christ's glorious presence will manifest itself out of you so that others will be drawn to Christ by the radiance of your daily lives. A big order! But praise God, we need more Church folks who will walk like Jesus walked, and who will talk like Him, and look like Him! God bless you Rox. My love in Messiah to all."

David was also one for sending very touching and beautiful cards. I have quite a collection. Each one always fit the situation; the "perfect card." I would often think, "Here I am running from store to store trying to find the right card, and David is in prison and has nicer cards than mine!" I once wrote to David, "I was searching and searching for the perfect card, but it was gone cause you got it. Ha!"

It was on April 28, 1995, that I opened an envelope to find David's very first card to me. I chuckled at the cover. A cartoon soldier stood with two shields covered with arrows, rocks flying about, and a juicy cherry pie about to fall on his head. The caption read: "Look at it this way...without these trials, testing of your faith, working on patience and fighting the good fight...life could be boring!" Mixed with the humor, however, was a serious message. David was keen to the spiritual battle that I was entering into by publicizing his testimony.

> "Dear Sister,
>
> Pray for the safety and protection of your loved ones, for the devil is determined to stop you. Keep on the full armor to stand against all attacks."

This was another side of David that I would also come to know—one that was somber and extremely serious. David Berkowitz was known worldwide as a Satanist. He had once been the prized trophy of Satan's army. Demonic forces had plagued him from child-hood. David never soft-peddled the reality of spiritual warfare, the ever-present battle between the angelic forces of good and evil. He wrote in another letter to me:

> "You must take my advice carefully; you are to keep on the full armor of God at all times; espe-cially now…because the devil is going to move. Make sure everyone is living a godly life with no grounds for any reproach. I am saying this because the devil hates me, and anyone associ-ated with me and/or helping me usually gets put through the wringer."

In a letter dated May 22, 1995, David wrote the following:

> "Hi Sister!
> I pray you and your family are doing well in Christ. He is the deliverer of our souls, the Keeper of Israel, and He never slumbers or sleeps."

Using his own special kind of humor, he then said to me:

> "I have several letters of yours to answer… I am going to get an old refrigerator to store your let-ters in. I'm going to need all that space. And once the refrigerator fills up, I'm going to ask for a sec-ond cell just for storage."

Then, almost as a pastoral reminder, he said:

> "Please take about ten minutes out of your busy schedule right now, Rox, to praise God and thank

Him. Take a few minutes to prayerfully read Psalm 95. Then make a joyful noise of praise to our God and meditate on Him and His goodness. This will strengthen and invigorate your daily walk with the Lord. Like a spiritual pep pill!"

This letter exemplified the David Berkowitz I came to know—a man of conviction and grace, a man of sincerity and joy, a man with eyes lifted toward the heavens and feet firmly planted on this earth.

Soon the time came for us to meet face-to-face again. Arriving back at Sullivan Correctional Facility took on a whole new flavor the second time around. This time, there would be no cameras, no lights, and no technical issues to worry about. The pressure of producing the "perfect show" was off. Would I see a different side of David Berkowitz?

After arriving and being processed in, the correction officer escorted us into the visiting room. My eyes swept swiftly across the room. It was nothing like I expected. Large unbarred windows loomed to my right, inviting daylight into the room. Instead of stainless steel tables and chairs bolted to the floor, small wooden tables and small child-like chairs greeted me. Against the wall stood vending machines filled with hamburgers, chips, popcorn, candy bars, various flavors of yogurt, and soft drinks, although I am very thankful for these wonderful machines. After many years of prison ministry, I now know that for inmates and their families, a regular visit, or celebrating a birthday or holiday means a few hours in a visiting room with vending machines that can never compare to the smell and taste of a home cooked meal, and the laughter and reminiscing that once took place around the kitchen or dining room table.

Two uniformed officers sat in the front of the room on raised platforms. We walked up to one of the officers, and I said, "I'm here to see Mr. Berkowitz." The officer then picked up the phone and announced our arrival. He then directed us to an alphabetized and numbered table where we would sit.

As we sat and waited, I scanned the room again. Glancing at the men's faces surrounding me, I couldn't help but wonder what they had done. What secrets lay inside their hearts? What lives were wrecked because of their crimes? Were they sorry? Did they care? My thoughts continued to escort me away. I was jolted back into the moment when the door from the prison hallway opened. Walking briskly with a big smile, David Berkowitz entered the room. He waved at us and headed toward the correction officers to check in. I stood up to greet him. As he walked toward me, I moved forward to give him a hug. Being the perfect gentleman, David leaned forward and hugged me around the shoulder, being careful not to cross any lines.

I introduced the friends that I had brought with me. David greeted each one, "Hi, bro!" while giving them a firm pat on the shoulder. Then we sat down together to talk.

CHAPTER 6

The Meeting

Sitting there in the prison visiting room, we certainly were an unusual bunch—a one-time rock n' roll star, along with a former drug addict, and an infamous serial killer.

Mike on the set of "The RoxAnne Tauriello Show"

Our conversation that day quickly turned from small talk to David wanting to know the backgrounds and testimonies of the men I had brought with me.

Mike, a one-time rock n' roll star, had tasted the fame and fortune of the showbiz world. With a gold album on his singing resume, he felt he was "on top of the world and had died and gone to heaven." On stage, he sang to crowds of ten to twenty thousand. Girls were giddy. People cheered. Fans even threw marijuana and bags of cocaine on the stage. After the show, women would line up, waiting for hours to meet him. He performed in huge auditoriums along with other celebrities. Mike thought he was invincible and that nothing could touch him.

On stage, Mike found a world of recognition and applause. Yet out of the spotlight, his world was spinning out of control. He struggled with depression. The let-down after a concert was like he had "just fallen down the bottom of a roller coaster." He said that on stage he was "high from all the adulation. You go from being on top of the world to feeling like you fell off the earth. Everything is a bummer. Nothing makes sense." Trying to fill the void in his life or at least numb the pain, he turned to drugs. He "smoked a lot of pot, snorted a lot of cocaine, and shot a lot of heroin." His life hit rock bottom.

Sitting alongside David was Rich, another Christian gentleman. Before coming to repentance and faith in Jesus Christ, his past had also been littered with drugs. In partial humor and disgust, he commented on the amount of money he had wasted, saying, "I snorted a brand-new Rolls and Cadillac up my nose." After coming to repentance and faith in Jesus Christ, drugs and waste were replaced with love and zeal to serve his Savior.

During the TV interview, David also recounted the road of destruction he had traveled on. Searching for something to satisfy the emptiness in his soul, he had gone from the casual use of drugs to the uttermost extreme—setting over a thousand fires, serving demonic forces, and committing cold-blooded murder. Recalling his days of youth, David said:

> "I remember when I was a young person. How confused and troubled I was. I didn't know that I was searching, but there was a cry in my heart; something that was not being fulfilled; something that just going out on a date with a girl,

or just getting high, or trying to do active mis-chief to create excitement or whatever to make life meaningful was just not cutting it…

You know the devil is truly a liar. He's so full of clever deception. He tries to create things that would give the flesh, a person's body, a lot of excitement and thrills, but what he doesn't tell them is that the ultimate price is death; that they are on a road, a broad road that leads to destruc-tion, and the devil blinds people. He blinds young people especially to the consequences of their sin. They don't fully understand the conse-quences of the life that they're leading; until they come to a place like this."

As I sat in the visiting room, I began to wonder to myself. "What really lies behind those doors, those doors that lead back into the prison world? Were there armed officers looking down, high above the prison population? Were there trained German Shepherds? How much violence was there between inmates? How many beat-ups, cut-ups, and slashings were there? How many shanks, (homemade weapons)?" Behind the prison door lay fear, guilt, anger, remorse, rage, loss of all freedom and control, the indignities of strip searches and the lack of all personal privacy. Your life is no longer your own. During shakedowns, correction officers turn over mattresses and go through all personal items searching for shanks, drugs, and other contraband.

Looking at the prison door each time I visited, I realized that it was more than just a door for inmates to enter or exit the visiting room. It was a door to a different world; a world of despair and hopelessness.

Mike understood. In 1975, he had been arrested for drugs. Then, three years later, as he was ready to release his second album, his lawyer called. "We've done all we can do, Mike. You have to come up for sentencing." What a jolt. "One day singing for crowds of thousands. You're signing autographs one day, and the next day you are handcuffed in the back of a police car."

Mike had also known the degradation of being processed into the prison house. "Everything, absolutely everything, from your shoes to your underwear…you can't even wear your own underwear! They take everything; your jewelry, your belt, your shoelaces. They give you state issued prison clothing, then they cut off all your hair. They give you a crew cut. They want to take away your identity." And the person is left with only a name and number.

Mike recalled the first time he was being walked to his cell. "Scariest thing that ever happened to me. Going down just looking. You would see a long row of cells. There's got to be forty of these cells just in a long, long row. It was just iron and cement. Cold. It was just like walking into death."

Mike's days and nights were filled with fear as inmates spoke in laughter and light conversations. "From cell to cell, they spoke of how many 'bodies' they had, (people they had murdered). It was a big thing. 'I have ten bodies…five bodies.'" Mike would later come to know Jesus Christ as his Savior and Lord. And after his release from prison, he would faithfully minister to inmates and be loved and greatly honored in his community and his home church, where the mayor and other high-ranking officials spoke on his behalf and celebrated a special day just for him!

As the conversation continued, I remembered how David also echoed the horrors of incarceration during my interview with him, saying, "Prison is a place where there's tension. There's anger so thick that you can cut it with a knife. Prison is the last place a person wants to be. Prison is almost like a type of hell. It truly is. There is hatred in this place. There is anger, fights all the time. From time to time guys get stabbed up."

As I looked at David, I could see the cold reality of it all. It was the infamous scar. Many years earlier, while incarcerated at Attica State Prison, David said, "A guy managed to 'sneak' me with a razor blade," causing a wound that required over sixty stitches, leaving him with a permanent scar across the side of his neck. Front page head-lines blared, "SON OF SAM KILLER SLASHED IN THE NECK AT ATTICA."

Suddenly, David got up and walked toward the front of the room. I walked to the window and continued to process all the thoughts in my mind. How much I take for granted! Walking back to our table, I met David in the middle of the room.

"Do you think you'll ever get out?" I blurted.

"Not unless God breaks down the walls," he answered.

David never once talked about getting out. His whole life was now wrapped up in ministering to the men he loved and served in the prison house.

Laying down before us were the Bibles he had taken from the table near the correction officers (for no inmate can take anything from the cell into the visiting room). David asked if we had any favorite scripture verses. I remember David saying that his favorite verse was Psalm 61:1 from the Old Testament. Then the next time he quoted Psalm 40:2 from the Old Testament as his "favorite verse." At first, I was perplexed by this apparent contradiction, but then I understood that David's love for God's Word was so great that almost every verse became his "favorite." Not only that, but David's knowledge of the Word was so extensive that he had the perfect verse for almost any occasion. Once while we were reading some verses from the Bible, he got so excited that he raised his hand, hit his knee, and joyful laughter flowed out of his mouth. The awesome power of God was not a "concept" to David. It was his lifeblood.

David was never ashamed to openly show his love and adoration of God. And neither was I. During each visit, we would always sing at least one hymn of worship right there in the visiting room. That very first visit David began to sing "Holy Ground." Not loud or boisterous, but in a strong yet tender way. This would become our hymn of choice, and we would sing it during our visits.

By now, it was twelve o'clock and time for lunch. We walked over and peered into the vending machines. I had come loaded with quarters thinking that David might need some change. I went to hand him some. Stepping back, he lifted up his hands and arms as if he was being arrested. Unknown to me was the fact that inmates are not allowed to touch or handle actual money.

During our visits, I was always concerned that David would have his fill of whatever he wanted. I often said, "How about another sandwich, a candy bar, or another soda? Come on, come on." After all, I am Italian.

After lunch, David and I would always sit there nibbling on popcorn. In our letters, I would jokingly write, "You know it's the popcorn that drives me up there. Ha!" But each time I went, I was always eager to share new ministry ideas with him, along with updates on what I was doing with his testimony on radio and TV.

As time went on, I got to know some of the correction officers, and we would share a few words before David's entrance into the visiting room. One correction officer, who had previously worked in David's unit, said, "I wish I had six hundred guys just like him." Another time, as I waited, I heard an inmate repeatedly banging on the door that led into the visiting room. I asked, "Is that David?" The officer replied, "No, David only knocks once." David Berkowitz was always the perfect gentleman, and was well respected and well liked, by both inmates and staff.

I remember seeing the results of an inmate progress report that David was given regarding his behavior while being housed at Shawangunk Correctional Facility. The report contained eleven categories that an inmate is evaluated on. Some of these include attendance and punctuality, attitude toward peers and authority figures, ability to follow rules and directions, effort and initiative, quality of work, self-control, and dependability. Marked next to each category on David's report was the word excellent.

During our first visit, all of us were sharing, talking and laughing. The time slipped by. We had almost forgotten where we were. It was now twenty minutes until three, and visiting hours would soon be over. David initiated a time of prayer. As we bowed our heads and he started to pray. I thought about him going back through "the door." He was no longer "Son of Sam" to me, but my dear brother in Christ. As we finished praying, the correction officer announced, "Visiting hours are now over." We then said our goodbyes. I knew that he was spending life in prison for the crimes he had committed, and rightly so. During the TV interview, in his own words, he said,

"I was worthy of the death penalty, and I was worthy to die for my participation in those crimes." But we also knew that David was a changed man. His body was still bound, but his soul had been set free.

That night, as I talked with my husband about our visit, one thing kept coming back into my mind over and over again. While sharing our testimonies, David, out of the clear blue sky, suddenly spoke about his childhood. As if staring back into his past, he said with glazed eyes, "When I was a kid growing up and I needed a baseball, my mom and dad always bought me the best. And if I needed a bat, they got me the best. And when I was growing up, they wanted me to be a doctor or a lawyer. But when I grew up, I became a criminal."

CHAPTER 7

Amazing Grace

What turns a person into a serial killer? Psychologists and sociologists generally scour through a killer's childhood to pinpoint the events and conditions that triggered his sinister side. Child abuse, neglect, and poverty often emerge as the likely culprits. But the story of David Berkowitz does not fit this mold.

On June 1, 1953, David Berkowitz entered the world as Richard David Falco. His biological parents were both married, but unfortunately not to each other. His mother, Betty Broder Falco, a Jewish woman abandoned by her husband shortly after the birth of their daughter, was a waitress desperately trying to make ends meet. His father, Joseph Kleinman, was a successful Long Island businessman who initiated an extramarital affair with the struggling waitress. However, when Betty Falco became unexpectedly pregnant, the relationship was jeopardized. Mr. Kleinman threatened to end the affair if Betty Falco kept the child. Emotionally torn, Betty eventually relented when she heard about a childless Jewish couple, Nathan and Pearl Berkowitz, looking for a child. The adoption was finalized and Nathan and Pearl welcomed the newborn into their home and renamed him, David Berkowitz.

David Berkowitz, happy and excited in his baby carriage

David's loving, adoptive parents, Nathan and Pearl Berkowitz

Nathan and Pearl showered David with love and affection. He was a beautiful baby with large blue eyes and black curly locks framing his cherubic face. Nothing would foreshadow that the answer to their dream would be a future serial killer.

David Berkowitz's father, Nathan Berkowitz, died at age 101,
and was a loving and faithful dad to David all the days of his life

Returning home from my visit with David Berkowitz, I could not shake his words about his childhood: "When I was a kid growing up and I needed a baseball, my mom and dad always bought me the best, and if I needed a bat, they got me the best. When I was growing up, they wanted me to be a doctor or a lawyer. But when I grew up, I became a criminal."

What happened?

During part 2 of the TV interview, I tried to connect the love of David's adoptive parents and the demonic forces that seemed to plague him even at an early age.

I asked David about his recollection of his childhood.

> RoxAnne: Now as a small child David were there demonic influences in your life?
>
> David: Yes, I believe there were. Looking back now…after I became familiar with the Bible, I saw in my life that I had many

of the symptoms of demonic possession. When I was a child, I would have all kinds of fits and tantrums. I'd hear voices.

David went on to describe childhood tantrums in which he hurled objects around the room and broke pieces of furniture. "Breaking furniture?" I inquired, picturing the chaotic scene in my mind.

> David: Yes, breaking furniture, and my parents were absolutely alarmed. They didn't know what to do with me. In school, I was constantly in trouble. The school staff there said I had to go to a child psychologist and made my parents take me there and so forth.

I asked David about a time in which a schoolteacher had to restrain him physically and force him out of the room.

> David: Oh yeah, we got into some tussle there and I created so much disruption in the class that the teacher got me in a headlock and threw me out of the room. I was totally unmanageable.

I continued the interview:

> RoxAnne: Now as a child, you were very depressed?
> David: Yeah,…for no reason. I had a good home, a good family, my mom and dad loved me very much, and gave me everything they could. Although we were, they were just hard working people. But I had bouts of depression where for days I would just hide in a closet or under the bed in the darkness. My parents didn't know what to do with me.

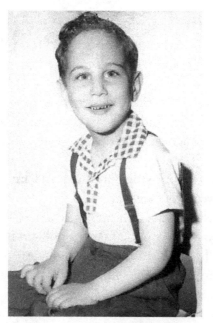

David Berkowitz as a child

RoxAnne: So you actually went into the closet and for hours you would seek the darkness.

David: Yes.

RoxAnne: For any apparent reason?

David: No, I was just a young child, five or six years old. I didn't know what was happening.

RoxAnne: To be in a closet. In the darkness?

David: Yeah.

RoxAnne: To be under the bed in the darkness.

David: Yeah.

RoxAnne: Why?

David: I don't know. I look back and I don't understand. At the time my parents didn't understand… But now that I see in the Scriptures that demons do possess children from time to time.

RoxAnne: Did you ever have an urge to flee from people?

David: Right, right, I just wandered the streets sometimes all night, coming home really late at night. Just wandered by myself.

RoxAnne: David, you said, and I quote, "I recall a force that would drive me into the darkened streets." Why?

David: Again, I look back and I see there were a lot of demonic forces in my life. I didn't understand that until I became a believer in Christ. At the time, I was just responding to impulses—things that would just take over and come upon me. [I would] just be off by myself wandering around in the dark.

RoxAnne: You also would feel very, very suicidal at times.

David: Yes. Well there were times when I would feel this tremendous urge—I was just like maybe ten or eleven years old at the time—to jump in front of moving vehicles—to jump out the window. We lived on the sixth floor in an apartment building in the Bronx, and there would just be these impulses, a tremendous pull, to destroy myself, to hurt myself in some way. And as I said, I didn't understand it until I saw, read it in the Scriptures. After I became a believer in Christ [I saw that] there were instances in the Bible where young children, for no apparent reason, would have the same thing come upon them and drive them into the fire, drive them to kill themselves too. In Mark 7 [of the New Testament] the story of the young girl that was demon possessed, and the mother went to Jesus asking for help. And in Mark chapter 9 there was the story of a young boy who was just totally possessed by demons, and he would throw himself into the fire and he'd be foaming at the mouth and going through all kinds of tantrums and everything, and the father wouldn't know what to do and cried out to Jesus Christ for mercy.

RoxAnne: Even while walking down the streets you said you felt this force wanting to throw yourself in front of a car? As I thought through those things I kept on wondering why David Berkowitz? Why you? Why?

David: I don't know. I don't know.

RoxAnne: Your parents would cry a lot.

David: Yeah.

RoxAnne: Try to do everything to change the situation.

David: Oh yes, I put them through a lot of grief, tremendous grief, because they didn't know how to handle me. They didn't know what to do. I was just wild, totally unmanageable, and my neighbors would constantly complain, and the local police would constantly seek my parents and say, "You'd better watch your child, and you'd better take care of him." And they did everything they could.

Wanting to warn young people and their parents, I asked,

RoxAnne: David what would you like to say to troubled teens?

David: RoxAnne, I would like to tell them that Jesus Christ loves them very, very much;

that He understands whatever problems or circumstances they may be going through; the hardships in life, and that He is the one that they have to turn to. The Bible says, concerning the devil, that he is a thief, and he comes to steal, kill and destroy, and it's really Satan and his influences in society today that are causing many young people to be so confused and troubled. They're getting surrounded on every side by so many demonic and satanic influences; but the Bible says concerning Jesus Christ, that "He has come that He might give life and that He may give life more abundantly". I remember when I was a young person, how confused and troubled I was because I was searching for something. I didn't know that I was searching for something, but there was a cry in my heart; something that was not being fulfilled; that just going out on a date with a girl, or just getting high, or trying to do some active mischief to create excitement and to make life meaningful, was just not cutting it. Now that I'm a believer in Christ, I understand that Jesus Christ came to give us a life full of hope, joy, excitement, peace, love, and mercy. Things that the world cannot give and I feel that a lot of young people need to be pointed to Jesus Christ. They need to be put on the path that leads to eternal life; that adults must keep pointing their children toward Jesus. That is what they need. That is the answer.

RoxAnne: And what about teens thinking about trying drugs? What would you want to tell them?

David: I want to tell them that once again, you know the devil is truly a liar. He's so full of clever deception. He tries to create things that would give the flesh, a person's body, a lot of excitement and thrills. But what he doesn't tell them is that the ultimate price is death; that they're on a road, a broad road that leads to destruction. The devil blinds people. He blinds young people especially, to the consequences of their sin. They don't fully understand the consequences of the life that they're leading. Until they come to a place like this. In prison, the walls will seem to close in on you. There is little room to walk around, and few places to let off steam. Prison is like a pressure cooker, and there are men who face time of ten, twenty, thirty, or more years, and the time passes slowly. Over the years, I have studied the sea of faces, walking the cellblocks and corridors. I see the vacant stares of lonely and restless men—men who live with little hope of a future.

David had been such a man. The first ten years of his sentence had been years of darkness, defeat, and despair. David described these years in a written testimony of his life, entitled "Hope" saying:

"I had no purpose for living, and thoughts of suicide filled my mind. I was bitter, angry, and miserable. I carried a "shank" with me just about everywhere I could get away with carrying it. A lot of guys were out to get me. I was living in a vicious cycle of kill or be killed.

A few years into my sentence, while I was housed inside the infamous Attica prison, a guy managed to sneak me with a razor blade, and I nearly died. With a sentence of 350 years plus life, and with no hope of ever getting out, I struggled to survive. Yet another part of me just wanted to die.

Maybe I should have been killed when the police surrounded me with guns drawn. They were more scared of me than I was of them. Back many years ago, in 1977 when I was age 24, and on a rampage for the devil, I felt as if I were ready to die. I was looking forward to a shootout. But it never happened this way.

I should have died when that inmate slit my throat. I should have died during many other situations in my lifetime. For I grew up in New York City (the Bronx) and was always in trouble. But God had other plans for me. Man, God has been good to me. I was a bona fide candidate for hell if there ever was one.

Yet for reasons that I cannot fathom to this very day, the Lord Jesus Christ made it His business to reach out to me with a love, kindness, and compassion that I have never known before. For the day came back in 1987, while I was walking the prison yard one cold winter's night, when another inmate walked up to me, introduced himself, and then boldly told me that Jesus Christ loves me and has a plan for my life.

After he said those words, I laughed at him and told him that there is no way God could love me. I told him I was too evil, that he was wasting his time. But this man, he had such a compassionate attitude. I cannot put this into words. Let's just say he had that special glow about him.

Although I rejected what he shared about Christ, for I knew he meant well, we became friends and started working out together. Every day he would quietly and patiently share God's Word with me. At first, I just listened politely. But after several weeks my attitude began to change.

One day he offered me a small pocket New Testament which included the Psalms. He urged me to read portions of it, especially the Psalms. Some nights I would peek into the Bible just to check it out. I wasn't raised in a home where the Word of God was read. So I knew next to nothing about what was inside it.

However, as I began to read from the Psalms, things began to happen inside me. I really found myself enjoying the words of the writers, especially King David. It seemed as if he were talking directly to me because my life appeared so similar. He was undergoing many trials and hardships. King David's life, to my surprise, had a lot of pain in it. Oftentimes he was surrounded by problems and trouble.

I said to myself, 'Hey, this guy really suffered!' I always thought that a king's life was supposed to be healthy, happy, exciting and prosperous. Yet I saw him cry out to God in his misery. I said to myself, 'I'm miserable too.' I was! But David's solution was to cry out to God for help and deliverance. Me, I used to cry into my pillow.

Then one day it happened. I was reading the Psalms late one night. It was close to midnight and I was alone in my cell. It was at this moment that my heart began to burst. The words I had been reading began to pierce my soul. Then everything hit me at once. The guilt, anger, the shame at failing my parents, loneliness, past hurts…everything! I began to cry like never before. I shut my light out, got down on my knees in the darkness of my little cell, and began to pour out my heart to the Lord. This was all new to me. Feelings of grief and remorse welled up inside me. I called upon God and talked to Him as if He were right in the cell with me.

I didn't even know if God was listening. But I just had to pray. And when it was over, I got up off my knees and it felt as if a tremendous load was lifted off me. This was the moment that I was 'born again.'… It was the start of a new life."

That day in 1987 something dramatic happened. No TV camera captured it on film. No media crew reported it on the late night news. But angels rejoiced. The Spirit of God transformed "Son of Sam" into a new creature.

"Therefore if any man be in Christ, he is a new creature: old things are passed away; behold, all things are become new." (2 Corinthians 5:17, NT)

After years of demonic influence, mental torture, depression, anger, and suicidal thoughts, David Berkowitz found what pills and self-help books could not do, and what psychiatrists and psychologists could not offer—forgiveness, a relationship with God, a new life. A life filled with God's peace, hope, joy, and purpose. David Berkowitz did not get what he deserved. Instead, he found mercy.

How can this be? David Berkowitz deserves to die. He deserves to be punished eternally for his crimes. In an article published on August 3, 1997, in the *New York Daily News*, Berkowitz himself even admitted, "I truly deserve punishment and death." But even if he were to die, his death sentence would not be "sufficient" punishment for the lives taken and shattered, nor for the grief and pain of family members and loved ones. David Berkowitz deserves the everlasting fires of hell. As stated earlier in his testimony, David realizes that he was a "bona fide candidate for hell if there ever was one." But again, even if he were to suffer a thousand years of torment, misery, and woe, it would still not satisfy God's wrath nor be able to pay his sin debt in full.

Yet David Berkowitz found the unthinkable. He found grace. But how can God forgive the vilest of sinners—a Satanist, an arsonist, a murderer? The answer can only be found in Jesus Christ, God's beloved Son. Being rich in mercy and abundant in grace, God sent his Son Jesus into the world to save sinners, to die in our place on the cross, to take our punishment for sin.

> *"For God so loved the world, that he gave his only begotten Son, that whosoever believeth in him should not perish, but have everlasting life."* (John 3:16, NT)

On the cross, God laid all of David's sins—the bitterness, anger, and rage; the filthiness and foulness of his thoughts and words; the evil deeds of his hands, the arsons, the murders, the blinding, maiming, and wounding of innocent victims, and every other sin he ever committed; along with the sins of omission, the good in his life he should have done but did not do—on Jesus Christ. On the cross, Jesus Christ became the sin-bearer and took the punishment and penalty for David's sins, being punished instead, in place of him.

> *"For he hath made him to be sin for us, who knew no sin; that we might be made the righteousness of God in him."* (2 Corinthians 5:21, NT)

And after three days, Jesus rose to show His power and victory over sin and death. This is why upon David's acknowledgment of his sins, and his desire to turn away from them and place his faith in Christ, his sins were forgiven, and all of God's wrath and future judgment were removed. Christ had paid David's sin debt to God in full. On the cross, before His death, Jesus cried out, "It is finished!"—paid in full.

Christ suffered and died on the cross not only for David Berkowitz's sins but for the sins of the world; for the sins of all of us. The cross of Christ is a wonderful story of God's love and an offensive indictment of man's sin at the same time. Now what I am about to say may sound shocking, yet from God's perspective, the question is not "how could God forgive David Berkowitz?" but "how could He forgive any of us?"

We are all sinners. We all fall short of God's sinless character and standard.

> *"For all have sinned, and come short of the glory of God."* (Romans 3:23, NT)

In leaping across a chasm, whether one falls a mile short or a foot short makes no difference. All die. All sin, therefore all are under judgment.

> *"For the wages of sin is death; but the gift of God is eternal life through Jesus Christ our Lord."* (Romans 6:23, NT)
> *"And as it is appointed unto men once to die, but after this the judgment."* (Hebrews 9:27, NT)

So why can't a loving God simply forgive? Why can't He overlook the "little sins" (like ours) and simply punish the "big ones" (like Berkowitz's)? Because God is a holy and righteous judge and He must punish the breaking of His law. No society honors a judge who punishes a few select crimes and winks at the rest. Such a judge is not heralded as a saint but denigrated as a crook. Besides, we are all guilty of the biggest sin. Jesus proclaimed that God's greatest command is,

> *"And thou shalt love the Lord thy God with all thy heart, and with all thy soul, and with all thy mind, and with all thy strength: this is the first commandment."* (Mark 12:30, NT)

Our highest obligation is to love God with every ounce of our being. We all disobey this command, whether our spiritual mistress is self-gratification, money, alcohol, drugs, illicit sex, or our own self-glory. We are all guilty of treason against our Creator.

Jesus is the only antidote for sin—the only cure from eternal condemnation. And just like a cure for AIDS (if one were to be found), the antidote works whether one is infected with the virus, and seemingly "healthy," or ravaged by it, and on the doorstep of death.

But like any cure, the medicine must be received before it can take effect. That night in 1987, David received Jesus. He acknowledged the multitude of his sins, was willing to turn away from them and embrace Jesus Christ as his Savior. When he did, new life began to course through his veins. "Son of Sam" died, and in his place "Son of Hope" was born.

CHAPTER 8

Media Blitz: "Grab the Sheets"

W hat a chapter title, but what a day it was. Little did I know that New York and New Jersey media crews would soon be swarming around my house with cameras and microphones. It all started the day before.

The David Berkowitz interview had just aired and as the credits flashed on the screen I smiled and breathed a sigh of relief. Just then, the phone rang. I picked it up to hear a news reporter from the *New York Post*. He was quite inquisitive and wanted to dispatch a photographer ASAP (immediately).

When the photographer left, my husband remarked, "Tomorrow you are going to have all the media here." I remember hearing him, but then again, he's the king of the one-liners, and his humorous remark just did not register.

Early the next morning, after seeing David's picture on the cover of the *New York Post*, the phone rang. A television news reporter was calling to alert me that he and his camera crew were sitting outside my home in the TV station's satellite van, waiting to come in and interview me. "What?!" As soon as I hung up the phone, guess what? It rang again...as a matter of fact, all the phones began to ring, and they rang and rang. They even filled up the voicemail.

"Hello, Mrs. Tauriello, this is Art McFarland from *Channel 7 Eyewitness News*, and I'm calling basically for the same reason everybody else is probably calling you today. I would very much like to talk to you and set up an interview on the same subject. And I would like to do it as soon as possible…"

"Mrs. Tauriello, this is Donald Berman. I'm with *Entertainment Tonight* in New York. I saw your story in the *New York Post*. I want to talk to you…"

"Hi, it's Peter Ward from *Extra*…"

"Andrew Edwards calling again from *A Current Affair*…"

"Hi, RoxAnne, it's Lou Young from *Channel 2*…"

"Hello, this is Celeste Ford. I'm a reporter with *WABC TV*. I'm calling back for RoxAnne Tauriello about your interview with Mr. Berkowitz. We are in your area. We are hoping to hear from you and we were trying to expedite but now we've come into this predicament where we haven't heard from you and we certainly hope that you'll be able to speak with us. I know you've granted some other interviews recently and we certainly would like to hear more about this. We are in your town."

"Frank Uciardo from *Channel 11 News*…"

"Hi there, Chris Murphy from *CNN*…"

"Hi, RoxAnne, this is Ed Speigel in addition to the long list of people who have called you…you will be getting a call from *Time Magazine*…"

Here I was walking around the house, coffee cup in one hand, my hair pinned atop my head, not a bit of makeup on, wearing a comfortable house dress, while the phone was ringing off the hook with major TV stations dying to interview me and on their way to my home.

I yelled to my assistant, "GRAB THE SHEETS! COVER THE WINDOWS!" We never did do that. After all, it was in a moment of frenzy.

I then called the prison and asked for special permission to speak to Mr. Berkowitz. I wanted to alert him about the article in the *New York Post*, which amazingly he already knew about. In prison, news travels fast. I was praying that we would be in agreement concerning my interviews with the TV media.

After explaining the situation to David, he said he would think about it, pray, and call back the following day. I thought to myself, I'm not getting the message across. They're here...and on their way. As we spoke, it was obvious that he was very hesitant. I knew that David truly wanted the gospel to be heard, but because I was still very naive concerning his past words to the media I didn't fully understand his fears. In the past, the man known as "Son of Sam," the .44 caliber killer, thirsted and thrived on sensationalism and hype. Would the reporters now take his testimony as stated so it would glorify the Lord, Jesus Christ? Or was this going to be a smear campaign, a mockery of the workings of Christ in his life? What about the families of the victims? How much pain would it ignite in their hearts? And what would be the ripple effect of all this media coverage? As the conversation ended, his closing words were that he was going to pray and call me back.

One of the many wonderful things that I have always loved about David is that his heart's desire is to always be in God's perfect plan and will for his life. He prays about everything. When David called back, his voice and manner revealed that he was still quite hesitant about the television news media. At times, when it came to the media, we were on a collision course, and Satan had a field day. Our backgrounds and views of the media were as different as night and day.

For me, the media was a blessing. Interviews with celebrity guests brought Christ-centered testimonies to the public's attention and free exposure for the programs, dates, and times. The media was also a Godsend for other Christ-centered events, especially *A Drive Through The Christmas Story*, which I had produced and directed for over thirty years. The media had given this event great recognition. *United Press International* had publicized it worldwide twice. And the major New York and New Jersey TV news media had come down to interview me and televise portions of the event, along with radio stations, and *The 700 Club*, which had come down twice. *A Drive Through The Christmas Story* had even made the front page of major newspapers in the area for years, bringing in tens of thousands to see and hear the gospel. For me, the media had been a blessing!

But for David, the media carried with it painful baggage about his past. Now almost beyond what he could bear. On August 22, 1977, the cover of *Newsweek* read "The Sick World of Son of Sam." Other publication's headlines read "Unmasking 'Son of Sam's' Demons" and "Sam Told Me to Do It… Sam Is the Devil," and on and on it went.

When my husband arrived home, satellite vans were parked up and down the block, and I was already in the process of giving an interview as other reporters and their camera crews waited by the door. My husband now took the lead, ushering and welcoming in one reporter and crew at a time. That day, as each reporter stepped into the living room, there wasn't one I did not recognize. My husband and I are "big time" when it comes to watching the evening news, and the networks had sent their top-notch people. As they entered, they quickly set up their camera and lighting equipment. Silently, I thanked God that I was not a novice when it came to dealing with the media or being on television. I was about to be interviewed by some of the sharpest reporters in the country.

As I sat face-to-face and eyeball to eyeball with one of the reporters, the first question out of his mouth was,

"What would you like to say to Stacy Moskowitz's mother?"

Stacy, a young, beautiful and vivacious woman, had been the last victim to fall prey to the murders.

Flashing back, I remember that my first question to David during my interview with him was about the murders. Although I didn't try to soft soap the horrible person he was then or what he had done, I also did not want to evoke painful memories and emotions. During another interview, with tears in his eyes, David Berkowitz spoke of young victims slaughtered as offerings for the cult's demonic gods. It was so horrifying to hear, that I did not want to enter into the unbearable pain and horror of it all. Something I would soon find myself doing during a radio program that was done live.

David was speaking from Sullivan Correctional Facility in Fallsburg, New York, while I sat behind the microphone at the station. The interview began with the question,

> "David, the crime spree you were involved in that brought terror to New York City, literally paralyzed New York with fear. In the aftermath, six people were killed, others were maimed. Looking back on this ugly, tragic time, what do you feel were the factors that led up to that spree?"

David responded,

> "Well, Andy, that is a very deep and extensive question. I was living without hope. I was involved in Satanism and the occult, and I had a really tormented childhood. I grew up in the Bronx always having psychological troubles. My family were loving parents, and I grew up in a Jewish home. I know that cruel demons had me bound since childhood. There were times when I was very suicidal and depressed. My parents had to pull me away from the window. The school officials used to send me to a child psychologist. People could not cope with me anymore, and it was just a matter of time before my whole life fell apart."

Andy then asked,

> "How do you feel about those who lost their lives
> and those who must live with the loss of a family
> member?"

As I sat listening, tears continued to well up in my eyes and to spill over. The microphone was beginning to pick up muffled sounds as David was saying,

> "Andy, I have no excuse. I lived like an animal. I
> was a diabolical devil. I know I ruined the lives
> of many people and I did Satan's dirty work. But
> now I look back and see that I was the biggest
> fool."

Emotionally like never before, I was facing the sin in his life, and the consequences it had brought on others. Thoughts of the victims, the parents, the pain and horror, God's amazing grace, and the David Berkowitz I now know, flooded my mind.

David continued,

> "I have nobody to blame, nobody to blame but
> myself, because I could have gotten out of what I
> was into, however slim the chances, I could have
> gotten out before it all began. I have nothing but
> deep sorrow in my heart…"

David was now choking up, holding back, trying to control his emotions and keep his composure, and fighting to continue on while I kept crying and crying. Yolanda, the producer, looking into the glass-enclosed room, and seeing how emotional I had become, left the control room to comfort me and bring me a handful of tissues as David continued pouring his heart out about his regret over all that had happened.

"I can't undo what was done. But in my heart, I wish I could just go back and change things... I will always continue to pray for the families who were hurt; not only for their own healing but that they would have the wonderful, wonderful privilege of knowing the God whom we know, knowing a wonderful and loving heavenly Father."

Now concerning myself, I would like to say from the bottom of my heart to each and every parent who lost a child, how deeply sorry I am for the death of your precious children, and for the never-ending sorrow and loss of all future hopes, dreams, and times you would have shared together; times that were so brutally stolen from you. Over the years, I am sure it has taken an unbelievable amount of love, determination, and strength just to get out of bed and go on living for the sake of your loved ones.

I am also deeply sorry for those victims who were wounded, and for each and every day of suffering, pain, grief, and anger you have endured as a result of these horrific crimes. I am sure that all of you would like to forget this living nightmare and hell, but you cannot. Berkowitz's name and face appear everywhere in the media and the brunt of his hideous crimes continue to slam you in the face.

It may also appear that I and others are trying to glorify him. But our prayers and our purpose is to use David Berkowitz's testimony and the gospel of Christ to reveal God's amazing love and mercy, because if God can forgive and change an arsonist, Satanist, and murderer—one of the vilest of sinners—then God is willing to forgive and change anyone! This is truly a message of hope! And if David and I can warn others about the consequences of unleashed sin and crime, and present the Savior, who died to forgive and transform lives, what future criminal may be turned from his sin before he acts on his thoughts? Who else will be saved from the ravages of addiction, prison, or suicide, and what other parents, families, and victims can be spared the unbelievable amount of sorrow and pain that you have endured?

As each interview ended, I walked the reporter and crew back to the satellite van, carrying with me footage of the Berkowitz show that the news media had requested to see.

David Berkowitz as he looks today

As I looked into the media van, I was put at ease immediately. It was almost like being in the control room at the studio, only this was much smaller and only used for on-the-road interviews. I handed the show over for insertion, and as soon as it was popped into the player, footage began to be laid down so they could choose clips of my interview with David Berkowitz to be inserted into the evening news along with the interview I had just given. As they looked into the monitor, they were taken by surprise as they noted the dramatic change in David's countenance and the words that flowed from his mouth. He was so dramatically different from the madman in the 1970s who had appeared on the news, with his hands cuffed and feet shackled, and an eerie smile on his face. They were now seeing God's new creation in Christ.

> *"Therefore if any man be in Christ, he is a new creature: old things are passed away; behold, all things are become new."* (2 Corinthians 5:17, NT)

I know for a fact that some of the reporters and crew gave serious thought to the possibility of God's transforming power as seen in the life of the former "Son of Sam." And as I said goodbye to each and every one of them, I did my usual thing and said, "Here's something good to read," as I handed them a gospel tract. Later that day, Lou Young from *Channel 2 News* left a message on my voicemail:

> "Hi, RoxAnne, it's Lou Young from *Channel 2*. It's a good move putting the machine on… I want to thank you again for your willingness to talk to us, and I do appreciate it. And I do. I did try to internalize all those things you told me and to get them on the air. Thanks again and I hope all is well with you, and I wish you luck with your show. Bye."

Now in the early evening, as the news began to air, my husband was in the rec room yelling, "Turn on *Channel 7*!" while I was in the kitchen saying, "Put on *Channel 2*!" Back and forth we went, watching all the different channels, from early evening till the late night news at eleven o'clock. How wonderful it was to see God's hand at work in the secular media. While airing the interview I had done that afternoon, they had also chosen to use some of my footage of David Berkowitz, the former "Son of Sam" now reading from the Bible, and expressing his faith and love in the Lord, Jesus Christ. That night the house was filled with "Hallelujahs" and "Praise the Lord."

The following day, *Entertainment Tonight*, a syndicated magazine show, called again asking for an interview. After agreeing to do the show, they dispatched a chauffeured car to pick me up while I arranged for a friend to accompany me to New York City. Today I would be speaking to people in Manhattan, Queens, Brooklyn, The Bronx, Staten Island, and all of America, shedding light on God's amazing grace and giving hope to those struggling in the depths and cesspools of sin, addiction, and crime. Using David Berkowitz as an example, that through Jesus Christ there is forgiveness and newness of life.

As I entered the door of *Entertainment Tonight*, the producer greeted me with a warm smile and an enthusiastic handshake. I was then led into the studio where everything was set up and ready to go. As I sat down, the interviewer and I shook hands, and within moments the interview began.

Afterward, I was ushered into the control room as excerpts from my interview with David were being fed to California to be put together, edited, and aired on *Entertainment Tonight* that very evening.

Riding home, I was on top of the world. I would soon be telling David that everything had gone so wonderfully. I would be fulfilling one of my goals for David, that being, to bring some joy into his life. For years, he had faced the horror of his crimes; day after day filled with pain and despair over the victims, and now I was so excited to tell him the great news. I had already rehearsed my words to him in my mind: "They even had you reading from the Bible and praising the Lord! David, people are beginning to believe what God has done in your life. What a message of hope!"

Months later, my interview with David Berkowitz would again be recognized by the media when I was invited to attend a gala affair at Trump Plaza in Atlantic City, New Jersey. The affair was the CAPE *(Cable Award for Programming Excellence)* and was being hosted by *CTN—Cable Television Network of New Jersey*, a station that aired my TV programs. As I held the invitation, my mind raced forward. Imagine if David and I won how happy he would be. In my heart, I felt that winning would be like a gift to him.

In order to be considered and to win the award, I knew the judges had to buy into the fact that David Berkowitz's testimony was real. Just think of the potential pressure and anger these people might encounter. The judges were all highly honored individuals among their peers and in their communities, along with being quite influential. Now, they would be putting their names, reputations, and stamp of approval on the line if we were chosen to take home the CAPE award.

The evening of the awards had arrived, and as the door to the ballroom opened, it was as if we were at the Oscars or the Emmys. The room was filled with an array of television producers, directors, writers, and camera, audio, and lighting technicians, along with heads of cable systems, politicians, and others. Everyone was dressed elegantly; men in black tuxedos, and women in long evening gowns and cocktail dresses. As I picked up a few hors d'oeuvres, I breezed around, joining in on conversations and saying "hello" to heads of cable systems and news anchors, as well as making new acquaintances. As the orchestra played, the evening dazzled, and the word for the night was "enjoy."

Following dinner, the time had come for the awards to be presented. As each category was announced, producers, hosts, camera crews, and their families were filled with anticipation.

The MC was now saying, "For best single program in the religion category..." Suddenly appearing on the screen was David and I. "And the award goes to '*The RoxAnne Tauriello Show/David Berkowitz Testimony.*'" I know I should remember my exact emotions, but I do not. What I do recall is hearing the orchestra play as I made my way to the stage. As I continued forward, it seemed as if time stood still. I was now standing on stage about to speak to hundreds of my peers. Tonight I wouldn't be reading from a monitor, cue cards, or hand cards. I hadn't even rehearsed a speech, yet I knew exactly what I wanted to say. I would be thanking God my Savior for my salvation and for the salvation of my brother David, along with my thankfulness for an incredible husband, family, director, and camera crew. I would also be doing what I love to do most; giving the gospel of repentance and faith in Jesus Christ.

> "*For I am not ashamed of the gospel of Christ: for it is the power of God unto salvation to every one that believeth; to the Jew first, and also to the Greek.*"
> (Romans 1:16, NT)

1996 CAPE AWARD "Cable Award
For Programming Excellence"

As I turned to leave I now held in my hands an award, not given by a Church or by a Christian organization, but given by the media industry. Amazingly, it was not given for an interview with a movie star or a humanitarian, but instead was given for an interview with a former serial killer who had experienced the amazing power of God's love, mercy, and forgiveness, and whose life had been totally transformed.

CHAPTER 9

From Murderer to Minister

We know that in the past, David Berkowitz was an arson-ist, a Satanist, and a serial killer. Then in 1987, he came to repentance and faith in his Savior, Jesus Christ, and for over thirty years he has been a servant of the Living God. I'd say that's a miracle. Wouldn't you? A miracle that only God can do!

Now, as time passed, David expressed that the following thoughts were upon his mind and heart:

> "God gave me a new name, the 'Son of Hope.' You're not going to be called the 'Son of Sam' anymore, that's when the devil owned you. But now you belong to me, my child, and you're the 'Son of Hope' and you're going to tell people about my loving kindness, you're going to tell people about my goodness, you're going to tell people that I am a merciful God, that I am slow to anger, that I am tender loving, like a father pities his children, so I have pity on people like you, David. And that's the message that you're going to proclaim…"

Now before I tell you how David serves the Lord, I'm going to tell you what he's really like, and the atmosphere and environment he ministers in, along with the amazing facts of how he touches lives here in America, and around the world. Then, as if you were a close friend of mine, I'm going to draw back the curtain and reveal "My Favorite Memories with David."

What is David Berkowitz like? David is truly a living example of God's love, mercy, grace, and transforming power in the life of one of the vilest of sinners. Today, as a child of God, David is constantly aware of his life, behavior, and actions before God and man. David is also a man of prayer who is extremely zealous in the area of evangelism. He has a great love for the saved and unsaved. He has great compassion and a deep concern and burden for teens, to warn them not to go down the road that leads to destruction—the path he was formerly on. I have found David to be humble, tender-hearted, and gentle due to the power of God in his life. The Bible teaches that he who is forgiven much loves much. David Berkowitz had set over a thousand fires. He had been a Satanist who worshipped and served the devil and his demons, as well as being involved in the murdering of six people, and the maiming and wounding of seven others. And yet he had received forgiveness from God.

How much love do YOU think David Berkowitz has for his Savior?

Today, David Berkowitz's whole being, his whole life is one of presenting his body as a living sacrifice. Serving Christ in every way is what David is all about. I have been saved for over forty-five years and I can say with a clear conscience before God and man that David is the most beautiful Christian I have ever met. Every Christian, in their life, behavior, and actions should be like David Berkowitz.

Now you may be saying, "RoxAnne, how do you know all of this? He's locked away in prison and you're on the outside." Well, let me give you my credentials. I have known David Berkowitz since 1994, and over the years, I have received over a thousand letters and cards, and even more phone calls from David, along with several hundred visits with him that lasted for hours at a time. I'm not someone who visited four or five times and decided to write a book about him. No, absolutely not! Some think of me as his best friend and right-hand person, while others say I'm his point of contact person. But in a letter written over twenty years ago, David said,

> "You are my sister in Christ, my friend in Christ, and my co-partner in Christ as we worship and serve the Lord together."

David Berkowitz and RoxAnne Tauriello spending one of many days together, as they share their thoughts and ideas concerning serving the Lord

Standing in front of a mural in the prison visiting room from left to right is Mark, David Berkowitz, and Roxanne Tauriello

Standing in front of a mural in the prison visiting
room from left to right is Pastor Steve,
RoxAnne Tauriello, and David Berkowitz

During phones calls with David, the majority of time is spent talking about how we are currently serving the Lord, and any new Christ-centered ideas or projects. During our visits, we continue to talk about serving God, as we fellowship and pray. Then David and I, along with my husband or a Christian friend, all have lunch together.

Now let me tell you, I'm Italian. Growing up, I spent quite a bit of time with my Italian grandmother, and during meals it was always "Mangia, Mangia" (Eat! Eat!). So when we go up to see David it's always, "Have another sandwich, more chips, another soda, a candy bar. How about some ice cream? Come on, come on." In a Mother's Day card David sent me in 2016, he wrote, "You've been mothering me for years." Of course these are words of endearment and no one could ever take the place of his beloved mother, Pearl. So now you can see that I know David Berkowitz extremely well.

David Berkowitz has many God-given gifts, talents, and abilities, including that of a pastor/teacher, which he uses as he serves the Lord. He is a true leader, and at times preaches in the prison chapel, as well as teaching Bible studies. He has the gift of encouragement which he uses as he ministers to inmates and others. He is also a gifted writer and uses this gift in personal letters, Christian journals, and newsletters. David is always about his Father's business, doing the work of an evangelist.

David has also started many new projects for the Lord, which include an outreach to Africa, and in the last prison where he was housed for twenty-eight years, he was well respected and started a unique ministry through serving the Lord in the mental health unit. At that time, David was the only person out of six hundred inmates allowed to minister to those who were mentally challenged. And there are many other good works that he does as well.

Only God knows the number of prison ministries that have been started due to his amazing testimony, and knowing him, along with numerous people who have been encouraged to pray for the salvation of their loved ones, realizing that if God is willing to forgive and save someone like David Berkowitz, then upon repentance and faith, God is willing to save *anyone*!

One of the ways David serves the Lord consists of answering the numerous letters that he receives from all over the world. Some come from people who are amazed at his testimony concerning who he was, how he was saved, the great transforming power of God in his life, and how he serves the Lord today. Others write because they too have heard his testimony, and they are desperate. They may be alcoholics or drug addicts, and because of their addictions, they have lost everything. They've lost their job, their spouse, and their children as well as extended family members, along with their homes and belongings. They've tried everything to break the chains and bondage of sin and addiction. They've read self-help books and attended self-help groups. They have been to psychologists and psychiatrists, taken prescribed medication, and even been admitted to hospitals or rehab facilities and nothing has worked. They are desperate and some are even suicidal.

Then, through a television or radio interview, a friend, a pastor, a Christian organization, or by reading his tract "Son of Hope: The Testimony of David Berkowitz", or by going on the internet to www. ariseandshine.org, they can read David's personal journal writings about his life in prison, his thoughts and feelings, and how he ministers to others.

People then write seeking help and David from within his tiny cell at Shawangunk Correctional Facility in Wallkill, New York writes back to them and gives them hope through the gospel; revealing that God is willing to forgive every sin, and that He is able to break the chains and bondage of sin and addictions. And that people's lives change through repentance and faith in Jesus Christ.

David has also written articles for Christian journals such as "The Woman's Christian Temperance Union" of S.D. and Christian Newsletters like The International Solid Rock Inc". Other requests for David's special writings come from pastors, youth group leaders, prison ministry volunteers, college professors and students, etc. Some of David's writings are also warnings for today's youth; not to go down the road that leads to destruction.

Speaking of these things, I put together a tract titled "David Berkowitz—Son of Sam—Son of Hope: The Interview," which includes David's testimony and writings about what life is like behind walls, bars and in tiny dungeons of doom, as well as a salvation message. This tract can also be found on my website www.roxannemin-istries.org.

David also touches lives through interviews he has done on radio and television including The Larry King Show and the Dr. D. James Kennedy program. There are videos of his testimony such as "Profiles in Faith", "Forgiven for Life", "Son of Sam Son of Hope", "The Choice is Yours", etc.

On my website listed above, look for TV on Demand where you can see The David Berkowitz Interview which won the CAPE Award, and some of my other television shows, along with the ministry to Africa, which David was responsible for starting, and the jail and prison ministries.

And here is something very interesting; David Berkowitz was asked to be the surprise guest speaker at the Suffolk Leadership Day of Prayer Breakfast by way of a video interview which was filmed in Sullivan Correctional Facility and played to those in attendance at the prayer breakfast, which included many high-ranking officials from Suffolk, Virginia. Following this, it made the front page of The Suffolk News-Herald titled "Suffolk Celebrates Day of Prayer—David Berkowitz Surprise Speaker at Breakfast".

Though there are many other things that can be said about David and how he loves and serves his Savior, I would like to close with this: a few years ago, the American Bible Society asked David Berkowitz to write a message for the "God Sets You Free Bible". These Bibles were to be used for jail and prison ministry and given to inmates. The message David wrote was entitled "Living With Hope" and it was placed on the front page of the Bible. Isn't God Amazing!

David's writings also include messages for pastors, youth group leaders, evangelists, and chaplains, which are read during church services and youth group meetings etc. They are letters and writings of encouragement to repent and trust in Christ, as well as warnings to today's youth, not to go down the road that leads to destruction. This includes alcohol, drugs, gangs, incarceration, possible suicide, death, and ultimately God's judgment and hell.

David also writes articles such as "Suicide is Everyone's Business," and "Alcohol—A Steppingstone to Prison." Vital messages as these can be found on the Internet at www.roxanneministries.org and ariseandshine.org.

As David works on these writing projects from within a tiny cell, which some call "Dungeons of Doom," he will be surrounded by drab cement blocked walls, along with a barred prison door—a constant reminder of where he is. His furnishings within the cell will be a bunk, with an extremely thin mattress, and a small metal locker where he'll put everything he owns. Anything else that doesn't fit will have to be put under the bunk. He'll also have a small sink and an open metal toilet, which is typical for jails and prisons.

As he works, you can be sure he won't be sitting behind a desk or on a cushioned chair. Absolutely not! Those luxuries are not found within the confines of the units or blocks where inmates live. Instead, he will sit on a bunk, trying to make himself as comfortable as possible. And of course, there will be no personal phone.

During the summer months, as he serves the Lord, he'll be sweltering in the heat, with no air-conditioning at all and only a tiny fan in his cell to help cool him off. And rather than a quiet library type of environment, all day long he will have to listen to buzzers, bells, and the banging of metal prison doors, along with loud talking, foul language, and at times, fighting, crying, screaming, and yelling, as he continues to write encouraging letters to others!

Now when David leaves his cell, like all inmates, his freedom of movement will be restricted. A prison official elsewhere, explained to me:

> "Everywhere you go you have to get permission. If you want to turn left, you have to get permission… I've been in prisons where there are lines, and you have to walk on a certain side of the line, and if you go over you are in trouble. Everything is pretty strict."

I remember commenting,

> "That's like being in kindergarten or first grade where the teacher has you walk together and start and stop. It is actually like being a child again. Is it true that at times, the inmates may even need to get permission to use the bathroom?"

He responded,

> "People say, 'I'm a man, I can do what I want to do.' You get in those environments and you don't do what you want to do. If you wanna go to the bathroom and you're out of your cell, you need to get permission. Some places shut the cell doors while everybody's in the day room and you have to ask the CO, your correctional officer. Everything is electronically controlled to open your cell again so you can go back in and use the bathroom."

Over the years, some people who don't know the reality of jail and prison have said to me, "Oh, Prison, it's a country club. They have TVs, they have gyms."

When you are incarcerated, all of your personal freedoms are taken away, including the freedom to make decisions for yourself. There are rules and regulations for just about everything. When to get up, when to go to sleep, when you can eat or watch TV, when you can have rec (recreation), a shower, a visit or make a call, and even what colors of clothing you can wear. Everything in prison is rationed out, from the jelly and the sugar, to the toilet paper. And if something else is given, usually something else is taken away.

Does that sound like a "country club" to you?

In jails and prison, you'll find that many are incarcerated due to the selling of drugs. On the streets and in the neighborhoods of America, they are known as drug dealers, or "The Man." The man that parents fear and kids seek to emulate. He's the man with the girls, the cars, the gold, the stash, and the gun. Some really make the big-time bucks and keep up with the times, going to the theater, and dining at the finest restaurants. But once he's busted and in prison, he's stripped of his street power and the opulence he once knew. So what does he have now?

In his cell, he will have an open metal toilet without a seat or a cover, a metal sink that runs only cold water, a small metal locker where all of his belongings are kept, along with whatever he can manage to squeeze under his bunk. All that he had once acquired and loved is now past history.

Gone are the girls, the cars, and the gold. Gone is the power and opulence. Gone are the good times, fancy restaurants, the greetings of maître d's, and the grand entrances. Gone are the reservations with the best table in the house. Gone is the gleam of crystal, sparkling champagne, and gourmet foods. Gone is the high life. It's all past history. His life surroundings now consist of fences, razor wire, bars, walls, and a dungeon with a toilet, a sink, a locker, and a bunk, along with lots of correction officers, and rules and regulations for every waking moment. This is his world and life now. This is what drug sales had finally brought "The Man."

In jails and prisons, where inmates are housed, they live in what is referred to as units or blocks that contain their cells. There is also an area for them to shower, along with a day room, which consists of some tables and chairs, and a phone or two that is shared by as many as thirty to sixty inmates. An inmate I interviewed at one facility spoke of the phone area as a hot spot, where fights can easily break out, and where a man can get "his wig split" (head cracked open) and a "chair upside his head" over usage of the phone. Most day rooms also contain a single TV. But can an inmate just walk up and flip on any show he wants? The bottom line is you get to see what you want to see if you have respect and strength and if inmates know you can muscle them around. Because in jail and prison power rules over those who are weak. You'll also find that all of your personal freedom and privacy is now past history. Even in the shower area officers have to look in to check that no one is trying to cut someone or hanging up (trying to commit suicide.)

When you're incarcerated you also lose your right to privacy. Correction officers monitor all areas of the unit or block, including even the shower, in case of a fight, or a suicide attempt.

Concerning this, an inmate that I had interviewed at another facility told me,

> "All your liberties, all your freedoms, privacy are taken away from you. You have a shower area that is opened up—officers have to be able to go in there…not always watching you, but in case they just have to take a look that no one's hanging up (trying to commit suicide), or getting into fights, or cutting each other or things like that they just have a chance of looking in."

From time to time the correction officers also perform "shakedowns." During a "shakedown," an inmate's cell is searched thoroughly from top to bottom for contraband such as drugs or homemade weapons, often called "shanks."

A prison official elsewhere informed me that

FROM SON OF SAM TO SON OF HOPE

"the prisons that have the most fear are the prisons
that have the most homemade weapons. There's a
lot of fear of inmate on inmate assaults. A lot of
people are fearful because they have heard stories
prior to coming in, about young guys coming in
and being raped."

Strip searches are another process that inmates must go through.
It can be a very humiliating experience for an inmate, but necessary
for the safety and security of the prison facility.

The same prison official also explained the process of a strip
search by saying,

"A strip search is not just stripping an individual of [all] his clothing, but it is actually having
the individual open his mouth. You look into his
ears. You shake his hair, or her hair, whatever the
case may be. You look into every body cavity that
there is. And the reason for this is, once again,
security, because these are places where drugs can
be hidden. People smuggle it into body cavities or
their hair, whatever. So a strip search eliminates,
or at least reduces the odds of this happening."

The bottom line is, you have to do what they say, even when
"the man with the badge" tells you to strip naked, squat and cough as
he checks for contraband.

Though shakedowns and strip searches are an invasion of one's
personal privacy, they must be done to remove all contraband (weapons, etc.) for the safety of the prison officials, and from inmate upon
inmate violence.

Every day, brave correction officers risk their own lives to help
reduce the possibility of violent confrontations in the facilities where
inmates are housed.

Even with shakedowns and strip searches, there is still a great
fear of violence in jails and prisons. Fights, cut-ups, stabbings, and

rape are not uncommon behind bars. I remember asking an inmate what the scariest thing was about being incarcerated. Their answer was "When you first walk in [they] yell 'Fresh meat'" I asked, "What do you mean?" Their response was, "Someone they can get close to, or take advantage of [sexually]."

I asked other inmates,

> "What is the scariest part about being incarcerated?"

They replied,

> "[You] have to worry about being cut or stabbed for no reason, because people in here, they do things on the spur of the moment...especially if you have a small piece of jewelry and they feel that they want it [they'll] do things like that for any piece of jewelry... You gotta do what you gotta do to survive... We cannot trust one another here... You never know [someone] could laugh in your face and still stab you in the back... Ya gotta watch your back all the time."

That's true, especially during the heat of the summer. In jails and prisons, inmates live in tight quarters with no air conditioning. These conditions create stress and tension that can lead to aggressive behavior.

Imagine you're incarcerated, and it's during the heat of the summer. There is no air-conditioning. No such thing as a fully opened window, a refrigerator, or a vending machine in the hall to grab a nice cold drink. You're with thirty to sixty other inmates, who have committed all sorts of horrendous crimes, including murder and rape, and like you, they are all sweltering in the summer heat. Many are short-tempered, angry, bitter, frustrated, hopeless, and depressed. And whether they are irritated or just looking for a violent confrontation with you, you'll find that in your unit or block, there is no place to hide.

Now, how is David able to endure living in such an environment?

Through repentance and faith in Jesus Christ, David has found peace, hope, joy, and purpose for life and living, as well as full assurance of eternal life in heaven. He also knows that God is always with him and will see him through any hardships, trials, or situations he may face.

> *"And the Lord, he it is that doth go before thee; he will be with thee, he will not fail thee, neither forsake thee: fear not, neither be dismayed."* (Deuteronomy 31:8, OT)

CHAPTER 10

My Favorite Memories with David

When it comes to serving the Lord, David is always extremely zealous in sharing the Word and witnessing to others. He is a very serious-minded person. However, over the past twenty-five years of knowing him, I have noticed that he also has a wonderful personality and a great sense of humor. During our many phone calls, letters, and visits, I have had the pleasure of experiencing moments of laughter and joy as we fellowship together. To illustrate this, I would like to now share with you some of my favorite memories with David.

During a conversation on the phone, I wanted to talk to David about some particular items I wanted to bring up to the prison for him.

As I began telling David about a particular item I wanted to bring him, his voice came back pleading and emphatic, "RoxAnne, please can't we just fellowship?!" David's whole life is about Christ and serving Him, and he just did not want to waste time talking about "things." I remember it took quite some time of me fussing and asking if he needed anything. Finally, a letter arrived enclosed with a list of several items. Jokingly, posted on all four sides of the page were the words, "Here is the list!"

Another time, after fussing again to bring him up something, he typed a short list, and on top of it he wrote, "Your favorite subject... shopping!"

In one letter, David wrote the following:

> "Praise the Lord! This is going to be a kind of short letter because I have to go to the chapel shortly, then I have a lot of chores to do (washing, ironing, and making up a nice 'HELP WANTED' sign for a permanent maid.)"

Another time, after sending reading glasses to David at Christmastime, he wrote,

> "In fact, the Lord used you to make a beautiful season for me. I got the glasses. They're great. I like the simple silver metal frame. It kind of matches my hair too." (Then jokingly, he wrote,) "I am seeing more gray these days, probably because you are making me nuts. It's the stress! Working with RoxAnne, ya know."

Once while doing a radio show, I determined that in the very beginning I would tell listeners about David Berkowitz and the dramatic changes God has made in him and his life. Over the microphone, I poured out my heart and went on and on. After the program aired, David surprised me by letting me know that he had heard the show. And speaking about my introduction of him, he said, "You sure laid it on heavy." And though everything I said was true, he made me break out into laughter. David is a Christian who is extremely humble.

Over the years, David and I have had many times of rejoicing. I remember one time while we spoke on the phone, I was telling David all of the wonderful things that were happening as we were serving the Lord. Unexpectedly he said, "RoxAnne, I have to go back to my cell and rejoice with the Lord." It was as if the praise was welling up so much inside of him that he needed an opportunity to let it out in a time of celebration to the Lord.

Another Christ-centered project we would soon be rejoicing over began when a Church, hearing of David Berkowitz and the outreach to Africa that he had started, surprisingly sent him thirteen boxes of Bibles and Christian books. Now these were good size boxes, and the cell he was living in was quite small, so who did he call? Me of course! And my response, after hearing about his dilemma was, "Send them to me!" When the boxes arrived, I began sorting and re-packaging all that was sent for a handful of impoverished pastors in Ghana, West Africa. They would be gifts. As the word spread to other servants of the Lord in Ghana, some began to advertise our outreach, not only verbally, but in newspapers and magazines, and the handful of letters from people requesting Bibles became many, and the many became a multitude.

Now, in 2010, Serge F. Kovaleski, a Pulitzer Prize-winning reporter from the *New York Times,* was interested in doing a story about David Berkowitz. It would be entitled "Guiding Berkowitz's Passage from 'Son of Sam' Murderer to Evangelical Christian". David asked me if I would assist in dealing with the reporter. As David and I were going back and forth with the reporter, I told him how David Berkowitz was the one who was responsible for having me start an outreach to Ghana, West Africa, to pastors, chaplains, Bible teachers and their students, to freely receive God's Word. He was so amazed that David could reach out and serve the Lord in this way, that over an extended period of time, he kept asking me, over and over again in many different ways, how David started this. David had said privately to me, and I agreed, "Wouldn't it be something if Serge asked you to spread those letters from Africa out on the dining room table, and then sent a photographer from the *New York Times* to take pictures." Well, guess what? That's exactly what happened. This renowned reporter, without a hint of what David and I had discussed, asked if I had the letters, and if I could spread them out on the dining room table so he could send a photographer. Amazingly, within the article, there appeared a large-size picture of one RoxAnne Tauriello, standing by the chandelier, next to the dining room table loaded with letters from Ghana, West Africa!

RoxAnne Tauriello and some of the letters from
evangelists, pastors, chaplains, Bible teachers, students,
and others crying out for the need to have a Bible.

One of the most wonderful memories I have with David happened during a time of great prayer. Over the years, David Berkowitz has been the only inmate—one out of six hundred men—allowed to go into the mental health unit to minister to mentally challenged inmates. He delighted in this.

In a letter, David wrote:

> "I just got back from our Thursday evening fellowship group at the mental health unit. It was a blessing as always… [I] told them that God wants to produce in their lives a faith that will carry them from day to day, from moment to moment, and even from crisis to crisis without

any of them having to fall apart mentally and spiritually. This is the victorious faith that God wants from us and gives to us…so we won't be losers and quitters but conquerors and winners."

In another letter, David explained to me in more detail how he helps these men:

"[I] help the men with their daily life coping needs such as cleaning, washing clothes, writing letters [to a loved one], etc. I give them encouragement to keep going as well as spiritual counseling. I encourage them to stay faithful to Christ or to turn to Christ. My short-term goals for them are to make it through each day without defeat, trusting in Jesus for help, strength, and spiritual guidance. My long-term goals are to see these men (who are Christians) get rooted and grounded in Christ, and to become stronger believers serving Christ with complete confidence in Him."

To help meet these goals, David's heart desire was to live within the mental health unit so he could be accessible to the men both day and night. In the mental health unit, there are times of grief and mental anguish, along with potential and failed suicides. This lay heavy on his heart, and I knew it.

In one of his letters, David wrote the following:

"We've been busy in the mental health unit and the ministry work never ends. There have been some nervous breakdowns, suicide attempts, fights and so forth. Please keep me in prayer as I seek to bring the light of the glorious gospel to these hungry guys."

One evening after we spoke, I hung up the phone and felt deeply burdened and very concerned about the whole situation. Going immediately to my husband, we prayed. Then following through, I also made calls to prayer partners and friends, praying with them and saying, "Every time you see me, I want you to pray for David. Please pray that he will be able to live in the mental health unit so he can minister there full-time." Then one evening, as I picked up the phone, I could hear the excitement in his voice as he said, "Guess where I am?" It is not like he is around the corner. He is in prison! He then blurted out, "I'm here in the mental health unit." Half screaming, I mouthed back, "You're in the mental health unit!" And we both broke into hilarious laughter, praising and thanking God. I could have jumped up and down for joy.

David now began confiding in me about his new cell and the former inmate housed there. "RoxAnne, you don't understand. The inmate before me had pornography everywhere. It was on the bed. It was under the bed. It was all over the walls." In prison, sex is often god. But amazingly, hanging in the middle of the wall was a cross. David believed that this cross amongst all of the pollution was a sign from God that he should be there. And on the cross were the words of Christ—"*I have come that they might have life.*" After reading these words, he repeated them over again. "RoxAnne, I have come that they might have life." That day, God not only answered David's heart desire but my desire also that David should live in the mental health unit to bring Christ's Word and love to needy men.

In another letter, he wrote:

> "It is the Lord Jesus who has given me His spe-cial touch for this unique ministry... I know that Christ has given to me a shepherd's heart for these men. I would like to think that some are doing better because of my presence. There are some wolves in here too. Let me tell you there are predators who try to devour the weaker ones... So I have to do some defending also. But this is part of my task. I'm really here because of love."

"This is my commandment, That ye love one another, as I have loved you. Greater love hath no man than this, that a man lay down his life for his friends." (John 15:12, 13, NT)

Shortly after this, I left on vacation, still excited and filled with thankfulness and joy. Upon arriving home, I opened a letter from David, and there it was before my eyes, a beautiful paper cross—the one that had hung in the middle of the prison wall; the one with the inscription that had read, "I have come that they might have life." In the letter, David simply mentioned:

> "Everything is going well in E-North and some of the guys are open to the Lord. These men have their struggles. I have learned to be very patient with them and to love them. I have my faults and weaknesses too. These guys, most have struggled all their lives with mental illness. Many had unstable homes where there was no love and no encouragement. They are the world's forsaken ones whom Jesus loves and died for. I too must love them and even die for them (John 15:12–14) [NT]. Well I have to go. Enclosed is the cross that was hanging on the wall of my new cell when I was moved in.
>
> Love in Christ,
> David."

I knew in my heart that he had parted with something that was of great significance to him, something that was cherished.

Another memory that I will always remember concerning how we served the Lord together, occurred during a cross visit. A cross visit happens when an inmate can invite another inmate out to the visiting room, so that they can visit together with the same family or friends. Here is how our cross visit came about. There were times when David would call and draw me more and more into his world and life. On the phone, he would say, "RoxAnne, I want you to minister to [Henry]," and the first question out of my mouth would be, "Is he saved?" Following this, David would also give me a brief description of the inmate's life. "RoxAnne, [Henry] has no one on the outside to call and no one ever visits him." In jails and prisons around the country, there are men and women who have absolutely no one. After years of addictions and trouble, their family and friends have forsaken them. They need a letter, a card, a visit, a voice from the outside that says, "I care."

> *"For I was an hungred, and ye gave me meat: I was thirsty, and ye gave me drink: I was a stranger, and ye took me in: Naked, and ye clothed me: I was sick, and ye visited me: I was in prison, and ye came unto me. Then shall the righteous answer him, saying, Lord, when saw we thee an hungred, and fed thee? or thirsty, and gave thee drink? When saw we thee a stranger, and took thee in? or naked, and clothed thee? Or when saw we thee sick, or in prison, and came unto thee? And the King shall answer and say unto them, Verily I say unto you, Inasmuch as ye have done it unto one of the least of these my brethren, ye have done it unto me."* (Matthew 25:35–40, NT)

David would then call out the inmate's name, saying, "Come to the phone. Sister RoxAnne is on it." And of course, ministering on the phone always meant, giving or making sure the inmate understood the gospel, along with words of encouragement to read the Word, listen to David, and see the example of Christ's love, peace, hope, joy, and purpose in his life. Now after ministering several times by phone to Henry, I would be meeting with him and David during a cross visit.

As we waited in the visiting room for Henry, David began to tell me how very alone the inmate was, and with tears in his eyes, he said, "RoxAnne, as a sister in Christ, I need you to show him a lot of love and affection."

But it would be during lunch that I would see David's love and the way he treated these mentally challenged men. As we sat eating with Henry, crumbs gathered around his mouth and chin, while some kept falling to the table. David, who today is as neat as a pin in every way, quickly leaped to his feet, grabbed some napkins, and like a loving father, gently began wiping away the crumbs from Henry's face. He then began to clean Henry's portion of the table. As I sat there watching and feeling the love he had for this man, the one-time "Son of Sam," who brutally killed and showed no mercy, now cared about others. Our God is a mighty God and is able to do anything.

> *"A new heart also will I give you, and a new spirit will I put within you: and I will take away the stony heart out of your flesh, and I will give you an heart of flesh."* (Ezekiel 36:26, OT)

Even though God is speaking to the nation of Israel, He places a new heart and spirit within each and every person who comes to repentance and faith in Jesus Christ. The Bible states, "Therefore, if any man be in Christ, he is a new creation: old things are passed away; behold, all things have become new." 2 Corinthians 5:17. God had performed this living miracle for David Berkowitz. He was a new creation in Christ.

CHAPTER 11

The Great Invitation

Today, even in prison David has peace, hope, joy, and purpose for life and living.

But what exactly does this mean?

Since coming to repentance and faith in Jesus Christ as his own personal Savior, David has found PEACE with God, because he knows that his sins are forgiven. He now has no fear of God's judgment and eternity in hell.

> *"Much more then, being now justified by his blood, we shall be saved from wrath through him."*
> (Romans 5:9, NT)

The word *justified* means being made righteous (just as if you never sinned) in the sight of God.

Through God, David also has a PEACE that passes all understanding in whatever situation he finds himself in.

Jesus said,

> *"Peace I leave with you, my peace I give unto you: not as the world giveth, give I unto you. Let not your heart be troubled, neither let it be afraid."*
> (John 14:27, NT)

The Bible also states:

> *"And the peace of God, which passeth all under-*
> *standing, shall keep your hearts and minds through*
> *Christ Jesus."* (Philippians 4:7, NT)

When it comes to HOPE, David has a *sure* hope, that upon death he will spend eternity in heaven with the One who loved him, and died for him, God his Savior. David knows that heaven will be a place of unimaginable beauty; a place with no tears, no pain, no sorrow, nor death.

The Bible states:

> *"And God shall wipe away all tears from their eyes;*
> *and there shall be no more death, neither sorrow, nor*
> *crying, neither shall there be any more pain: for the*
> *former things are passed away."* (Revelation 21:4,
> NT)

David also has the JOY of knowing God through His Word, and through his own life experiences. And like the apostle Paul, no matter what trials come into David's life, he feels great joy in preaching the gospel and caring for the needs of others.

> *"But none of these things move me, neither count*
> *I my life dear unto myself, so that I might finish*
> *my course with joy, and the ministry, which I have*
> *received of the Lord Jesus, to testify the gospel of the*
> *grace of God."* (Acts 20:24, NT)

As he prays to the Lord, God hears and answers his requests, giving him the desires of his heart, in accordance with God's perfect plan and will for David's life. And no matter what circumstances he finds himself in, David can always count on the sure promise of God, which states:

> *"And we know that all things work together for good
> to them that love God, to them who are the called
> according to his purpose."* (Romans 8:28, NT)

David's PURPOSE FOR LIFE AND LIVING is to glorify God through his new life in Christ, by his behavior and actions toward God and others, as he proclaims the Glorious Gospel and zealously serves the Living God.

> *"And he said unto them, Go ye into all the world, and
> preach the gospel to every creature."* (Mark 16:15, NT)

And what are David's thoughts about the day when he will stand before God, his Savior, concerning his new life in Christ as a servant of the Living God? Speaking from his heart he said,

> "The greatest words I can ever hear from the lips
> of my Savior is, 'well done thou good and faith-
> ful servant. You've been faithful in little that I've
> given you to do. Enter into the joy of the Lord.'
> I'd say, thank you, Jesus. You're truly a wonderful
> God. You're truly a wonderful Savior and Lord."

You may be thinking, how can I receive God's forgiveness, a relationship with Him and eternal life in heaven, along with God's peace, hope, joy, and purpose for life and living?

The sad fact is that most people believe they can receive these gifts from God through keeping the Ten Commandments. But what does God say in the Bible? Concerning all of mankind, God states these words:

> *"For there is not a just man upon earth, that doeth
> good, and sinneth not."* (Ecclesiastes 7:20, OT)

"As it is written, There is none righteous, no, not one." (Romans 3:10, NT)

"For all have sinned, and come short of the glory of God." (Romans 3:23, NT)

These Bible verses reveal that all of mankind is sinful and therefore breaking God's commandments.

Now, maybe you're wondering...if the Ten Commandments aren't the way to heaven, why would God have given these laws? God, through His servant Moses, gave the Ten Commandments to Israel and to us, as a guide to our everyday life, behavior, and actions. The Ten Commandments reveal to us what God is like, that He is holy and righteous. These same laws reveal that we are sinners. The Ten Commandments also point to the need for something else to save us; that being Christ Jesus.

"Wherefore the law was our schoolmaster to bring us unto Christ, that we might be justified by faith." (Galatians 3:24, NT)

What about having a "so-called" good heart as a way to enter into heaven?

The Bible states:

"The heart is deceitful above all things, and desperately wicked: who can know it?" (Jeremiah 17:9, OT)

What about doing "so-called" good works or deeds as a way to please God and therefore enter into heaven?

Concerning this, the Bible states:

"But we are all as an unclean thing, and all our righteousnesses are as filthy rags; and we all do fade

as a leaf; and our iniquities, like the wind, have taken us away." (Isaiah 64:6, OT)

Nor can we be saved by anything else but through the person and the work of Jesus Christ—His death, burial, and resurrection.

"Knowing that a man is not justified by the works of the law, but by the faith of Jesus Christ, even we have believed in Jesus Christ, that we might be justified by the faith of Christ, and not by the works of the law: for by the works of the law shall no flesh be justified." (Galatians 2:16, NT)

"Neither is there salvation in any other: for there is none other name under heaven given among men, whereby we must be saved." (Acts 4:12, NT)

Simply stated, a name represents a person, place, or thing. And the Bible says there is *no* other name; whether it be a person, a certain religion, a certain place, or commandment keeping; a "so-called" good heart, works or deeds, or anything else, that can save you from God's judgment and hell.

Now let me show you a real-life story found within the pages of the Bible. It is an actual account that took place as Jesus hung upon the cross. And it will reveal, beyond a shadow of a doubt, that a person cannot be saved and earn a home in heaven, by doing good works, deeds, or anything else except through repentance and faith in Jesus Christ alone. We find this absolute truth described in Matthew chapter 27 and Luke chapter 23.

The Bible states:

"Then were there two thieves crucified with him, one on the right hand, and another on the left. And they that passed by reviled him, wagging their heads, and saying, Thou that destroyest the temple,

and buildest it in three days, save thyself. If thou be the Son of God, come down from the cross. Likewise also the chief priests mocking him, with the scribes and elders, said, He saved others; himself he cannot save. If he be the King of Israel, let him now come down from the cross, and we will believe him. He trusted in God; let him deliver him now, if he will have him: for he said, I am the Son of God. The thieves also, which were crucified with him, cast the same in his teeth." (Matthew 27:38–44, NT)

"And one of the malefactors which were hanged railed on him, saying, If thou be Christ, save thyself and us. But the other answering rebuked him, saying, Dost not thou fear God, seeing thou art in the same condemnation? And we indeed justly; for we receive the due reward of our deeds: but this man hath done nothing amiss. And he said unto Jesus, Lord, remember me when thou comest into thy kingdom. And Jesus said unto him, Verily I say unto thee, Today shalt thou be with me in paradise." (Luke 23:39–43, NT)

The last words that Jesus said to the thief on the cross are amazing! *"To day shalt thou be with me in paradise."* After all, this man was a criminal, and he was dying because of a wicked lifestyle of sin. So what did he do to deserve or earn eternal life in heaven? Nothing! But he did do that which is necessary to enter into heaven. On the cross, he repented. He admitted that he was a sinner when he said to the other thief the following words. *"Dost not thou fear God, seeing thou art in the same condemnation? And we indeed justly; for we receive the due reward of our deeds..."*

Notice that instead of hatred and anger because of his suffering on the cross, the thief realized that he was worthy of punishment and death because of the sinful life he had led. He also drew a contrast between himself and the sinless Son of God. Referring to Jesus, he says, *"But this man hath done nothing amiss."*

FROM SON OF SAM TO SON OF HOPE

God, in His love, mercy, and grace, opened the eyes of this man and he realized that the one crucified beside him is no mere mortal man, but God the Son, and even though he saw Christ nailed to a cross, suffering and dying, he believed that Jesus would be a king over a kingdom, and after calling Christ "Lord" he said, *"Remember me when thou comest into thy kingdom."*

Now let me ask you, what did the thief do to deserve heaven? Once again, he did nothing. His previous lifestyle was why he was being put to death. But he did that which God requires. He repented. He acknowledged that he was a sinner. And the all-knowing God, who sees into the heart, knew this man's desire to turn away from sin. Then, revealing his faith in the Savior as the only one who could give him eternal life in heaven, he said, *"Remember me when thou comest into thy kingdom."*

And because of his repentance and faith in the Savior, the Lord answered him with these amazing words. *"Verily I say unto thee, Today shalt thou be with me in paradise."*

Now had the thief been able to come down from the cross, his whole life would have changed. Why? Because upon repentance and faith, a person receives the Holy Spirit, whose work in every believer is to transform them into the image and likeness of Christ. And now, out of love for God his Savior, he would have desired to love, obey, worship, and serve his Savior, not to get into heaven but because he was going to heaven.

So how can YOU escape God's judgment and hell, and receive His forgiveness, fellowship, and eternal life in heaven, along with His peace, hope, joy, and purpose for life and living?

YOU MUST REPENT. You must come to God with a sorrowful mind and heart concerning God and sin, accompanied with a desire to turn away from a lifestyle of sin, the attitude and actions that offend a holy and righteous God.

In the Bible, Jesus said,

> *"Except ye repent, ye shall all likewise perish."*
> (Luke 13:3, NT)

YOU MUST BELIEVE that Jesus Christ was and is God, the Son.

> *"In the beginning was the Word, and the Word was with God, and the Word was God."* (John 1:1, NT)

> *"I said, therefore unto you, that ye shall die in your sins: for if ye believe not that I am he, ye shall die in your sins."* (John 8:24, NT)

YOU MUST BELIEVE that Jesus Christ was and is God The Son, and that He is the Savior, the one who took the punishment for our sins.

YOU MUST BELIEVE that upon the cross Jesus Christ took personally for you, God's wrath—the punishment and penalty due to you and your sins.

Speaking of the crucifixion of Christ upon the cross, the Old Testament states:

> *"They pierced my hands and my feet. I may tell all my bones: they look and stare upon me. They part my garments among them, and cast lots upon my vesture."* (Psalm 22:16–18, OT)

Also in the Old Testament, the prophet Isaiah revealed these words concerning the crucifixion:

> *"But he was wounded for our transgressions; he was bruised for our iniquities: the chastisement of our peace was upon him; and with his stripes we are healed. All we like sheep have gone astray; we have turned every one to his own way; and the Lord hath laid on him the iniquity of us all. Yet it pleased the Lord to bruise him; he hath put him to grief: when thou shalt make his soul an offering for sin, he shall see his seed, he shall prolong his days, and the pleasure of the Lord shall prosper in his hand."* (Isaiah 53:5, 6, 10, OT)

And in the New Testament we read:

"Who his own self bare our sins in his own body on the tree, that we, being dead to sins, should live unto righteousness: by whose stripes ye were healed." (1 Peter 2:24, NT)

YOU MUST BELIEVE that Jesus Christ died for you, was buried, and on the third day, He rose from the dead. The very moment you come to God with true sorrow for your sinfulness, with a desire to turn from sin and place complete trust in the Person and Work of Jesus Christ as God's only way to Heaven, God will forgive all your sins, past, present, and future. You will have a personal relationship with Him and God will now hear and answer your prayers giving you the desires of your heart in accordance to His perfect plan and will for your life. Through the tribulations of life, all things will now be working together for good, and upon death, you will spend eternity in Heaven with the One who loved you and died for you, God your Savior.

Right now, if you would like to receive God's forgiveness, fellowship, and a brand-new life free from the chains and bondage of sin and addictions, along with eternal life in heaven, David and I would like to invite you to bow your head and say these words to God if you mean them with all your heart. Remember that it is repentance and faith in Jesus Christ as personal Savior—not words alone—that save you.

"Lord, I know I am a sinner. I am sorry for my sins, and by your enabling power, I desire to turn away from sin. I believe that Jesus Christ was and is God the Son, and that He died on Calvary's cross, taking the punishment and penalty for my sins so that I will not be punished in hell. He died, was buried, but on the third day rose from the dead. I now receive Him as my own personal Savior, knowing that through Him alone I receive your forgiveness, a relationship with you and eternal life in heaven. Thank you, God."

If you've just prayed this prayer and meant it with all your heart, this is God's promise to you.

> *"These things have I written unto you that believe on the name of the Son of God; that ye may know that ye have eternal life, and that ye may believe on the name of the Son of God."* (1 John 5:13, NT)

> *"For God so loved the world, that he gave his only begotten Son, that whosoever believeth in him should not perish, but have everlasting life."* (John 3:16, NT)

In closing, David and I pray that you have come to know the True and Living God as your own personal Savior and Lord, that you will grow in loving obedience to Him, that you will find a Bible-based Church where the Word of God is preached in all truth, and that you will be a mighty servant, proclaiming The Glorious Gospel until His return.

What great things He hath done
Maranatha!

ABOUT THE AUTHOR

RoxAnne Tauriello has gained national and worldwide recognition as a television talk show host and a producer of special events. Over the years, she has interviewed various people, from sports celebrities to pastors and entertainers. She has also interviewed those who were formerly addicted to alcohol and drugs and who now give glory to Jesus Christ for forgiveness and deliverance from the chains and bondage of sin and addictions, along with a brand-new life and eternal life. *The Roxanne Tauriello Show* can be seen on cable television, YouTube, or online at www.roxanneministries.org.

CPSIA information can be obtained
at www.ICGtesting.com
Printed in the USA
LVHW040247180723
752707LV00009B/177